Carlisle Writers' Group

WRITE AGAIN!

Dedicated to
our families and friends

Edited by Neil Robinson and John Nevinson

Cover illustration by Hayley Cordley

Contents

The Valentine
Out Of The Frying Pan, Into The Fire
The Mysterious Mr Bentley

The Mist
Legend Has It...
The House That Karl Built

Elsa's Choice
Carpe Diem
Overheard In An Old Churchyard

Sanctuary
Transition
Work In Progress

Twisted Fate
Life's Cycle
When Green And Red Make Beige

The result of flash-fiction exercises, some themes – 'A Moment In Time' and 'The Clock Struck One', for example - are addressed by more than one author.

Foreword
by Matt Hilton
author of the Joe Hunter thrillers

I was never a member of a writing group, but how I wish I had been! For a long time, while writing alone, I tried unsuccessfully to find like-minded people - other aspiring authors - to befriend. I recall visiting libraries and asking if they knew of any local writing circles or groups I could join, but I never managed to find one. I'd have loved to be involved in a group back then, if only to share advice, ask and answer questions, talk about writing and read out my work for peer feedback, but it didn't happen for me.

Back in 2008 my name caused quite a buzz in the publishing world when after a hard fought auction between a number of large publishing houses, I was awarded a five book deal and record breaking advance for a debut thriller author. My overnight success was viewed with equal measures of excitement and envy by other aspiring authors, and established authors for that matter too. People wondered how a policeman from Cumbria, with no contacts in publishing whatsoever, managed to crack the system and become such an overnight success. Some people decided that I must have had the golden touch, huge amounts of luck or, as one critic even suggested, I must have been sleeping with an editor.

The truth is that my overnight success came on the back of decades of writing, submitting and suffering rejection. My 'debut' novel was actually my ninth completed book, and alongside those nine I'd probably written and discarded about ten more, plus numerous short stories and articles before I finally found a formula that met publishers' expectations. When I finally got my deal I was 42 years old, and had been constantly writing since about the age of eleven, so you can see that, no, I didn't have the golden touch, wasn't lucky in the least, and believe me, I wasn't sleeping with an editor or anyone else outside my marital bed! All I had was persistence, and an undying dream. I worked hard at learning my craft, took the knocks along the way, and kept going. Now when I look back over those thirty plus years I see them for what they were: me serving my time, learning my craft and finding my individual voice.

Although those years were well spent, I now look back with some sense of regret that it took so long, and that I spent so many hours in seclusion while tapping away at my latest work. Much of that time happened before the advent of the internet and social networking, and some people might find it hard to believe that prior to getting that deal I didn't personally know another author, had no contacts in publishing, and everything I did was through a process of trial and error (mainly error). Back then my only resources were 'how to' books and magazines that I gleaned for advice, and a copy of the *Writers' and Artists' Yearbook* through which I'd seek agents and publishers, marking them off as each turned me down. Because I'd no contacts, I had no one to offer me answers to simple questions that some people might take for granted these days. I remember fretting over a simple phrase 'no unsolicited manuscripts', and wondering what on earth that meant, but I had nobody to ask.

Without knowing the parlance or industry speak, I had no clue what it was telling me. I thought, how can any book sent blindly not be unsolicited, so wherever I saw that phrase I simply didn't bother sending my work to the recipient. I know it sounds ridiculous now, but when you don't know, you don't know.

With all that said, you can probably imagine my delight when I was recently approached by Carlisle Writers' Group, who kindly invited me to one of their gatherings to talk writing and publishing. I was thrilled. It gave me the opportunity I was looking for all those years to meet and chat with people with similar aspirations and dreams of publication. I've now had nine books traditionally published, and been included in a number of anthologies, but my ambitions have never changed. I still want to write, and I still have questions and answers, and to me there's no better way of talking them through than with your peers. If some of the things I've learned along the way could prove beneficial to those in the group I was more than happy to share.

And what a great bunch of people they were. They were welcoming, enthusiastic, innovative, creative, and humble: my kind of people. They were a mix of all ages, sexes, and demographics, with a wide range of interests and influences and their writing styles reflected that diversity. Carlisle Writers was set up with an ethos that has never changed: to support and encourage writers in what can sometimes be a lonely occupation. I can certainly attest to that last, but finally feel as if I've come in from the cold.

Carlisle Writers is made up of aspiring writers, poets, and

novelists, some already published, some of who write only for pleasure, all of them talented. They regularly give readings of their work to community groups, and have collaborated on previous anthologies, and on the occasion of my visit had recently published a collection called *Write On!*, a copy of which they kindly presented to me. While I was with the group I was honoured when asked to write a foreword to their next collaborative effort. The very book you are now clutching in your hands.

So here you have it: *Write Again!*

In this collection you can expect short stories, flash fiction, and poetry across a wide range of genres, all written with the individual and unique voices of the authors. You will laugh, shed a tear, feel your pulse quicken or the hair creep on the back of your neck, reflect in contemplation, or grin in triumph, but mostly you will enjoy the reading experience, and isn't that exactly what we want from any writing? Some of the writers' names might be unfamiliar to you, but that won't last. Who knows, perhaps one of the authors herein is destined to be a household name, the next big thing. One thing I'm positive of is that with such a supportive peer structure behind them, and the proof of their talents right here in this book, they will continue to produce terrific, imaginative writing for many years to come.

Enjoy!

Matt Hilton

Introduction

Carlisle Writers was formed by a handful of people in the 1990s, with a view to helping and supporting writers of any ability. Now meeting every first and third Monday each month at the RAOB Club on Fisher Street, we still support and encourage writers in what can sometimes be a lonely occupation.

Some write for pleasure only, while others aim to publish their work. Many members are already published poets and novelists, but still like the friendly and informal atmosphere of the meetings.

We often share our work in anthologies such as this and by giving readings to various groups in the community. I do hope you enjoy this new anthology of our work; you can find out more about us on our blog at www.carlislewriters.blogspot.com

Thank you for your support.

Marjorie Carr

Chairperson,
Carlisle Writers' Group

June Blaylock

June joined Carlisle Writers' Group three years ago and is retired. She appreciates the friendship and support of group members as well as the occasional theatre outings and visits from guest speakers.

June's interests are many and varied; chief among them is writing poetry and short stories, which she does purely for pleasure and to keep her brain alert.

The Valentine

'In the spring a young man's fancy lightly turns to thoughts of love.' So wrote the poet Tennyson, and the imminence of St. Valentine's Day on February 14th gives both young and old the opportunity to send romantic messages to the object of their affections - although the outcome may not always be what they expected!

Joyce, a single mother, was shopping with her daughter Annette in a large department store in town, when suddenly Annette stopped and blushed scarlet. She was very excited.

"Look Mum," she said, tugging her mother's sleeve. "There's Austin Campbell. Isn't he just gorgeous?"

So this was the Austin she had heard so much about. The boy was tall and slim, wearing the latest designer tracksuit and trainers. His hair was brushed up in the latest style and he had a piercing in his eyebrow. He wore black nail polish and had a gold medallion round his neck. He nodded condescendingly as he swept by.

"Well, I don't know what's so special about him," said Joyce.

"But he's so good at everything; sports, maths, history and things, and he's deputy head boy and everybody likes him!" said her daughter.

"Well, I think he's a bit..." Joyce realised suddenly that she was talking to herself. Annette was nearly swooning behind a pillar, talking to her friend on her mobile phone.

"Yes, I've just seen him," she breathed, furtively looking over her shoulder. "He's just lush. He's getting into the lift now. I bet he's going down to the music department. Oh, he's so, so, hot!"

Annette caught up with her mother. "Can I get a Valentine's card and send it to Austin?" she said. Joyce smiled. She too remembered having crushes on slightly older boys. She recognised in retrospect that some of them would have been patently unsuitable as partners. At fifteen, her young daughter was suffering the pangs of growing up.

"Well, all right," she said, "but you don't have to sign it, you know. You don't even need to include a message."

Annette bought the biggest card she could find and when they got home she read it over and over again. On the front there was a mountain with a perky little person on top. It read, "I hope you are not embarrassed that I sent you an over-the-top card but ..."

When the card was opened, the little person had fallen over and rolled down the mountain with the words, "I just couldn't stop myself! To the most amazing, gorgeous, wonderful person!"

The day before Valentine's Day Annette rushed home from school, "I've found out where he lives. Please, Mum, will you deliver it for me. He won't recognise you if he sees you and I can't send it through the post because I'm sure he knows my writing!"

"Where does he live?" said Joyce.

"31, Willow Tree Crescent. You know where the path cuts through from Willow Tree Crescent to the main road? Well, his house is half of the semi next to the cut." said Annette.

"Oh, all right," Joyce agreed. "I don't often get to walk through the posh end of town as it's a bit out of my way."

The following morning Joyce made a diversion on her way to work. She found the cut and the house with number 31 on the gate next to it. She was surprised that it looked a bit run down, but glad that it was only quarter to eight in the morning. It was still barely daylight and everybody's blinds were drawn. She pushed the card through the letterbox and thought there was a faint flicker behind the curtains as she closed the gate. Maybe it was just her imagination.

She went through the cut and was glad when a bus stopped and took her directly to town, dropping her off near the library where she worked.

Joyce worked steadily throughout the morning. First there were the newly returned library books to put back on the shelves, then some posters to arrange on a huge display board promoting 'Thirty Ways To Save The Planet'. As she walked to and fro she became aware that someone was watching her from a table in the reference department. An elderly man was sitting there; she had seen him in the library many times before, but today he had been there all morning. He tapped the table leg to attract her attention and she went over.

"I'm sorry to interrupt your work but I just wanted to say I think you are the most amazing, gorgeous and wonderful person too," he whispered. Joyce noticed that his eyes were dewy and his nose was running slightly as he fumbled for his handkerchief. "And don't worry about being embarrassed about going over the top, although it took me right back to my days in the war. I didn't know you knew - about the medal I mean." He got up to go and limped towards the door.

"Well, goodbye, my dear. Now you know where I live, you can call at my house any time." He patted her shoulder and left.

Joyce was puzzled. This is the funniest thing that has ever happened to me, she said to herself.

Just then the chief librarian came out of his office. "I think Major Fortescue-Brown has got his eye on you," he said. "He's actually a very brave man. Did you know that at nineteen he was the youngest lad ever to be awarded the Victoria Cross? He was dug in, manning a machine-gun post on top of a hill in Italy near a monastery where the Allies had evacuated their wounded men. The rest of his mates were killed around him and when he was shot in the leg, he just tied a tourniquet round it and continued to fight. His bravery saved dozens of lives."

It dawned on Joyce that some mistake had been made and on her way home she decided to go down Willow Tree Crescent. There at each side of the cut were the two semis, at one side numbers 31 and 33 and at the other side 35 and 31. No! That should be 37 but the top of the seven had cracked off and looked like a one. She had delivered the card to the wrong house! Even as she stared in disbelief, the front door opened and the old man appeared with a red rose in his hand.

"I didn't expect to see you so soon," he said smiling. "Please take this. And I just want you to know you have made an old man very happy!"

Joyce was making tea when her daughter came home. "Austin never said anything to me," said Annette, looking rather subdued. "He was too busy with a crowd of adoring girls." Then she brightened up. "But Nigel Thompson has asked me to go to the cinema on Saturday and I didn't even send *him* a card. He said he doesn't mind. He's really lovely! It's funny how things work out, isn't it? I don't think Austin was worth it!"

"Neither do I," said her mother fondly, "but I know who was!"

Out Of The Frying Pan, Into The Fire

The sound of sobbing could be heard coming from the kitchen as young Lady Eleanor D'arcy Beaumont strode furiously down the upper corridor of Bartridge Castle. Before her servants scattered and fled, flattening themselves against the wall in the forlorn hope of becoming invisible.

She entered her private apartments and flung the door shut, hurling herself into a nearby chair. Old Esther, her lady's maid, turned from smoothing the covers of the tapestry-covered four-poster bed and asked, "Whatever is the matter?"

"Well, I've sacked the cook for a start," she replied. "I think she must be trying to poison me; for three days I have been sick and never want to see another goose again. And then there's my dear husband Herbert, who thinks of nothing but hunting, riding and drinking. By night time he's hardly ever sober. I will not sit back and be told to take up embroidery and singing. I want something more from life. I want my freedom!"

Esther's mouth fell open. She had some sympathy for Eleanor. At nineteen she was a strikingly beautiful young lady with golden hair and blue eyes. Moreover, she was vibrantly intelligent and self-confident. The Earl was more than twice her age; her father had arranged the marriage to him, one of the conditions being that the Earl would cancel her father's many debts. Love had not entered into it, but to ask for her freedom – that was unthinkable!

"Bring me pen and paper, Hetty, I intend to write my husband a letter telling him that in the three years I have spent in his bed, I consider I have earned my freedom. I want nothing from him now but to consider myself single."

Hetty placed the writing materials before her, trembling. "I do hope you know what you are doing," she said. "Have you considered the consequences?"

Eleanor did not reply. She was engrossed contemplating the vellum, each sheet headed by the family crest and motto: *In vinculis etiam audax* - 'In chains yet still free'. At a stroke she crossed it out, writing above in capital letters: *NON IN VINCULIS IAM LIBERA SUM.* 'Not in chains: I am now a free person!'

Having composed the letter to her satisfaction, she sanded and folded it, holding a block of sealing wax to the guttering candle. A huge blob of blood-red wax fell onto the flap and she stamped it with the seal. It was done.

"Now, I want you to get ready and be waiting for me at the postern gate in ten minutes," she said to Hetty. "I wish to visit Widow Hoskins whom I have heard has the gift of foretelling the future. I want to know what it holds. But first I must deliver this letter to the Earl."

"Your ladyship," replied Hetty, "I have heard that Widow Hoskins deals in witchcraft. I cannot countenance entering her house."

"Then you will have to wait outside!" said Eleanor tersely, pulling on her cape.

His Lordship, Earl Herbert D'arcy Beaumont, was to be found in the drawing room, sitting - or rather lying spread-eagled - in a chair by the open fire. His balding grey head was thrown back and a loud rasping snore emanated from his open mouth.

The fact that the goose had been fat and greasy appeared not to have bothered him at all; in fact several remnants and stains could still be seen on his linen shirt and doublet. What had concerned him was the fact that his favourite Spanish wine had run out during dinner and he had had to supplement it with several flagons of ale. An empty tankard lay on the table before him.

His favourite black-brindled hound sat upright beside him, its muzzle snuggled into his lap, occasionally licking the limp hand. Eleanor stealthily lifted up the tankard and slipped the letter underneath it before tiptoeing away.

A twenty-minute walk brought Eleanor and Hetty to Widow Hoskins's dwelling. During the walk, Eleanor had relaxed and confided to Hetty that she had fallen in love with a young man she had met while out riding and was prepared to risk anything to be with him.

A stout hawthorn hedge surrounded the garden of Widow Hoskins's humble wattle and daub cottage. Several weeds were peeping through it and many other kinds of flowers were blooming there. Eleanor pushed open the wicket gate and walked towards the open front door. The room seemed sparsely furnished with a table, a couch and a wooden cupboard. Clothes hung on hooks around the room.

"Come in, I have been expecting you," said a quiet voice.

Widow Hoskins was not as Eleanor had expected. She was tall

with white hair and rosy cheeks and a smiling face. She looked piercingly at her with big brown eyes.

Suddenly the room began to spin, she felt giddy and knew no more until she woke up to find she was lying on Widow Hoskins's settle.

"You have fainted," said the quiet voice. "What brings you here?"

"I have come because I have been sick every morning and again this evening since eating goose. I also need to know what the future holds, because I want my freedom."

"I wonder if the sickness is the result of you being with child, rather than because of anything you have eaten," said the widow sitting down beside her.

"If I may examine you, I can confirm this for you". A few minutes later she gave her the diagnosis:

"There is happy news; I can tell you that you are definitely pregnant. The sickness will go of its own accord within a few weeks, but until then eat only food that is light in texture."

"But I have sacked the cook!" said Eleanor.

"May I suggest that you re-engage her and make her privy to your secret? She will see it as a privilege and a measure of her skill to provide such dainty morsels as are nutritious and appropriate for your condition. Your second problem is more difficult as there is no such thing as complete freedom. Every beggar and orphan will tell you that at its most basic, freedom entails responsibility, if only for one's own health and safety."

"But *you* have freedom," said Eleanor. "What is *your*

responsibility?"

Widow Hoskins pushed open the door.

"Here is my garden: in it grows peppermint for indigestion; echinacea for colds; evening primrose for rheumatism; lavender and marigolds for swellings and itching and St John's Wort to soothe frayed nerves. The bark of the white willow tree relieves pain and fights fever; even the dandelions, nettles and foxgloves in the hedgerows have an ailment they cure. It is my responsibility to guard and pass on the knowledge of their properties for the benefit of future generations - and for this I risk being tied to a stake and consigned to the flames!"

Eleanor was silent. In Widow Hoskins she had met her match.

"Is your wish for freedom anything to do with the young knight I have seen languishing for you at the wood's edge every evening these past weeks?"

Eleanor nodded. "And what is his name?"

"His name is Sir Myles FitzHerbert and my heart dances and sings whenever I see him. I met him two weeks ago when I was out riding and he helped me home when my horse went lame. I cannot live without him and I will be with him whatever the consequences. But my husband is the father of this child."

Widow Hoskins smiled and stood up. "I am neither judgemental nor am I a gossip, your secrets are safe with me. You wished to know your future, so I will give you this riddle to work out as you go:

Mother Nature's work is done,

The son will be father to his father's son!"

Eleanor told the riddle to Hetty who was waiting at the gate for her. She hugged her before going to meet her lover.

Hetty made her way back to the castle and peeped into the drawing room. The snoring had stopped but the hound was whining and pawing his master's knee. The Earl seemed to be asleep but his eyes were open. The letter lay unopened under the tankard. Hetty felt his pulse then took the letter and put it onto the fire, watching it burn, before gently closing his eyelids with her fingertips and pulling the bell cord.

Suddenly there was the sound of running feet and stunned voices relaying the news that the Earl was dead.

Hetty looked through the window of her turret bedroom. The Earl's personal standard had been lowered and was flying at half-mast. A servant had been despatched to light the huge beacon on Bartridge Tor; soon the whole shire would know of the Earl's demise. She could see the tall-lighted candles in the chapel and the chaplain hurrying to undertake the all-night vigil. Tomorrow the Earl's tenants would file past his body to pay their respects, gaping in awe at his robes and coronet.

Death had afforded him the dignity he had not had in life for some time!

A horse clip-clopped through the portcullis gate. They were coming back! It was Sir Myles FitzHerbert leading Eleanor on his big black horse. He tenderly lifted her down, supporting her with his arms as they walked towards the chapel.

Hetty had solved the riddle for herself. If she was not mistaken, this was Myles, the illegitimate son of the Earl, who would stand in *loco parentis* to Eleanor's child. There was now no reason why Eleanor should not marry the man she loved, but would he gradually become like his father? Had Eleanor jumped out of the frying pan and into the fire? Or would their love and her strength of character forge the most successful partnership Bartridge Castle had ever known?

But answer came there none, and all was silent save for the mournful howling of a broken-hearted hound.

The Mysterious Mr Bentley

Mr Richardson carefully reversed his new van into the meagre space in front of his small terraced house and looked back at it with satisfaction. The sign writers had done a good job: 'Nick Richardson Plasterer – Quality cornice, coving and tiling undertaken,' he read.

As he turned the key in the front door he could hear the telephone ringing.

"Hello? That you, Nick? It's Drew MacDonald here." It was a local builder.

"Hi Drew. How's things?"

"Well, I need a favour. Have you seen our board outside what used to be Bentley's on Abbey Road? It was two old Victorian houses in poor condition, but we're doing them up and we've knocked them into one property for a client. There's going to be an antique furniture showroom on the ground floor and a Victorian-style café on the first floor and what's now two attics will be one big store room. We've had to move a staircase and brick over a door. . ."

"Yes," said Nick, wondering whatever was coming next.

"Well, the ground floor's nearly finished. The painters are in there now and I had plasterers in on the first floor but they've jacked it in and left me in the lurch!"

"Why?" asked Nick.

"Well, that's a mystery. To be truthful, one of them fell off a ladder and broke his ankle - the ceilings are very high, you know. He said he didn't know how it happened; the ladder just seemed to suddenly topple over on its own and it wasn't his fault, but I think they'd been larking about and hadn't secured it properly. Anyway, they're not coming back and it's left me in a predicament. Please Nick, can you finish it off for me? It'll only take you a day or two."

Nick thought for a moment. He didn't like taking over someone else's job. But on the other hand, he did have a new van to pay for.

"Yes, all right. I'll start on Monday morning," he said.

Monday morning came and Nick arrived in good time to see what the job entailed. He could see where the accident had happened, just where the staircase had once been. He fastened his planks securely onto a scaffolding platform that he had brought with him. He was not going to risk falling – it was an occupational hazard among plasterers and builders.

The day passed quickly and Nick quite enjoyed his work. As a quality tradesman he could appreciate the craftsmanship in the beautiful ceiling roses, ornate plaster cornices and ornamental Greek-style architraves. The original features would be left.   It would make a lovely Victorian-style café.

He sat down to have his packed lunch. Suddenly the door creaked and flew open. An icy draught blew through the room, lifting his packet of crisps off the bench where he was sitting and scattering them across the floor. Nick felt the hairs on the back of his neck stand up and he shivered. He could hear the painters' voices echoing in the empty room below and above him in the attic there was the sound of thumping and hammering; someone was dragging a heavy piece of wood across the floor.

On Tuesday the painters finished downstairs and before leaving carried their paint pots, ladders and dust-sheets up onto Nick's floor. They would have to wait for the plaster to dry out for a week or so before coming back to decorate it.

"Have we got people working upstairs?" Nick asked one of the painters. "Yes, I think so," he replied, "but I haven't seen any of them. They're not a very sociable bunch."

With the painters gone, an oppressive, eerie silence descended. Nick felt uneasy. It was creepy being alone in the house and he was glad when it was half past five. He went into the room at the back of the premises for his coat. It was in what had once been the cupboard under the stairs and his trained eyes noticed that here the original wall had had a wattle and daub construction. This part of the building was much older than he had been led to believe.

As he got into his van, he glanced back at the top floor attic windows. The joiners were evidently still working. There was a dim pale blue light flickering, as if they were working on emergency power and he could see a man's face silhouetted at the window. He waved and was amazed to see the man shake his fist at him before turning and disappearing into the gloom.

Nick was interested in finding out more about the building's past. So he decided to call in at the library on the way home. He borrowed a book on the local history of the town and discovered some very interesting information.

The property on the right had been an inn in the eighteenth century and a stout Georgian building had stood next door, the home of a Mr Isaac Bentley. This Bentley had been a rich wool merchant who had evidently become a recluse after his wife and baby son had died from smallpox. There was a painting of Mr Bentley in the book; he had been mayor of the town in 1775 and despite the white curly wig and tri-corn hat Nick immediately recognised him as the face of the man at the window.

It was rumoured at the time, that apart from one precious, gold half-guinea that he always kept in his waistcoat pocket, Isaac had hidden all his money under the floorboards in the attic. One night, two highwaymen staying at the inn had broken into his home and attacked him. The old man had threatened them with his stick and in the struggle that ensued they had pushed him down the stairs. He had died later. The highwaymen took up the floorboards, found the money and escaped on horseback. They were soon apprehended, tried and eventually hanged.

Nick got little sleep that night and decided that in the morning he would go straight upstairs and see things for himself. He knocked at the attic door and then pushed it open, cautiously peering inside. He gasped; the whole room lay undisturbed, deep in dust, cobwebs and empty boxes. There was a hole in the floor but no sign that any workmen had ever been working there.

Nick stood dumbfounded amid the debris and dust. He suddenly felt deeply sorry for the lonely old man who had once lived there and said softly:

"Don't worry, Isaac, old chap. You can rest in peace. They got them and the money in the end."

He turned towards the door to leave. There was a slight sound behind him. A box had been dislodged by the vibration of his footsteps and something was rolling towards him. It was a coin. It spun round and fell at his feet; he picked it up and put it in his pocket.

There were no further incidents that day and undisturbed, Nick quickly completed the rest of the work and locked up. On his way home he returned the book to the library.

"Is there anyone here who can tell me what this is?" he asked the librarian, taking the coin out of his pocket and handing it to her.

"I'll just go and see," she said. A moment later she returned with Philip, a very excited local historian.

"This is a very interesting find. Where did you get it?" He asked.

"From an old house I've been working on," Nick replied.

"Well, it's an extremely rare George III gold half-guinea, dated 1774. Very few were made that year, so it's worth a great deal of money. This one is in mint condition. We may even consider buying it for the museum here. Would you like to sell it?"

Nick thought for a moment - after all he couldn't spend it himself and the money would go a long way towards paying for his new van - but who did it actually belong to?

"Yes, but only if the previous owner agrees," he said.

"And who might that be?" asked Philip

"Well, possibly the very mysterious Mr Bentley!" said Nick and they laughed.

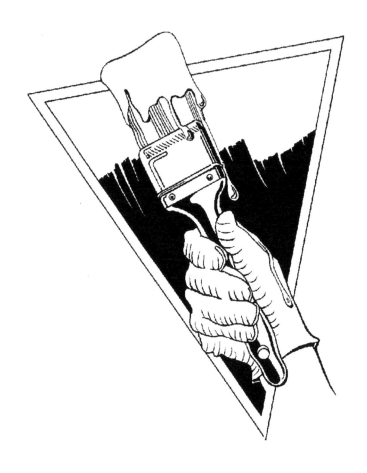

Nick Robinson

Nick has been a member of the writing group for two years and revels in the ideas which the medium offers. He has always enjoyed imaginative activities.

He is originally from the Midlands but moved to Cumbria, which he loves, eleven years ago. Recently, he has studied English, sociology and psychology at university and is currently training to be a teacher.

The Mist

It was three years to the day when the mist came down. At first, I hardly noticed the change but day by day the mist grew stronger until eventually it completely enveloped me. The funny thing about mist is that it is very difficult to know where you're heading or where you are, how far you've come and what is happening to you. Standing on a high peak with cloud all around soon messes with a person's sense of direction; any half-decent walker resorts to a compass to aid their aimless wandering. I wish I had had a compass to find my way!

On good days the mist almost lifts completely and the bright sunshine feels good and hot on my shoulders, the birds sing merrily and the leaves on the trees glisten in the morning dew. Senses come to life; I can smell home-cooked bread, freshly cut grass and smoky bonfires burning in the distance; my vision becomes acute and I can see intricate patterns and little eddies in the river; reflections bounce up at me, entering my soul. My energised body feels golden and electric from the brush of the breeze or the caress of a lover. It is on days like these that the mist is forgotten about and is confined to a corner of my consciousness.

But it remains; it is never banished entirely, lurking in its deep, dark pit waiting,waiting, waiting... Waiting like a pack of hyenas until its prey is weak, laughing and braying. The hyena never goes for the outright kill but takes pleasure in letting its prey suffer and decline before the brutal massacre begins.

Bit by bit, the enthusiasm and spirit dwindles until I am just a shell, a dried-out husk. I lie in the darkness, the mist surrounding me on every side, trapping me until I can hardly breathe - a cruel suffocation of the mind.

But I am not dead; it just feels that I am. Lifeless and worthless, I'm floating on a body of water, drifting out away from the security of the land and into the wasteland of the sea. Bobbing helplessly, I do not fight and do not swim for the shore. It's as if I'm paralysed, drifting aimlessly away from friendly smiling faces and hopeful thought.

There is no pain in the mist. It's strange to want something that hurts when you're ill, but at least with pain there is a feeling of *something;* something real that can be identified with and can bring you back to the world. A symptom to show that there is a problem. In the mist there is no such relief. Surely a padded cell awaits me as I rise from my bed and I eat breakfast in the silence of the long room, looking forlornly out the window. People come and go and conversation is maintained but I find no pleasure in it. It is a means of getting through the day. Routine is best when thinking is unwelcome and there is no pleasure in reading.

Time is for the busy and the lively; I am neither of these. In the mist, I forget about time as it seems irrelevant, far away from me on my island of gloom. The clock ticks on endlessly and I sit and fester, my life drifting into the future.

One day, I wake like any other and the phone is handed to me. I listen to the words that are being said to me but I'm not really listening. I just think I'm listening. The mist has me in its grip but from somewhere the message plays in my hollow head as if on an old, rusty gramophone, echoing and reverberating. The message says something about 'mental illness being okay and that it can be treated.' The mist is deep and yet the words have found me and make sense. There is a rumour of logic about them and history plays its part. I rise and make the call.

I sit in the waiting room. I feel nothing and I say nothing. There is no one around and I wait. I hear the doctor say my name and I get up as if in slow motion from my chair and walk into a small office that has no particular interest to me. I sit and stare across the table at a woman I do not know. She asks me what the matter is and I look at her. Something stirs within me and I start to talk slowly at first but then faster and faster until finally she stops me. I feel the tension breaking and tears well up in my eyes. She has guessed, and I'm relieved that I don't have to play the game any more. The secret is out and this is the start of something. I feel hope rising in me.

I have my antidote, I tell myself, looking at the green and yellow capsules on my rough, grey hands. I quiver and sink them down and that is that. I wait. I feel nothing at first and no change seems to have taken place, and then I feel hissing in my head as if something is being released. Something is happening I can feel it now, I feel lighter. The mist is lifting slowly; day by day, hour by hour, minute by minute, something has changed; a light is now on and I feel I'm returning home.

It's difficult to measure change when things happen so slowly. Although the mist has lifted and light re-enters my body, there has never been a pivotal moment or a monumental shift. All I can say is this is how I was and this is how I am now. It's almost like waking from a dark dream which happened long ago in the past. I'm looking back on it as if it had never happened or was maybe just my imagination.

And the mist? Well, the mist has lifted but I still feel its presence on the periphery, a reminder of what has been and what may be again. It's a part of me still, forming my character, shaping my words, damping my thoughts but I'm aware of it and in control. This is everything.

Legend Has It...

Merriment was rife in the long room, but Svenson the Red was not in the right spirit for the party that surrounded him. Supping his dark mead, he looked wearily around the dimly lit hall, nodding and grunting to his brutish peers. On his table, Svenson ignored the jovial jests of Lars Blue Tooth, a large oily-skinned Norseman, and a sly-faced Dane named Horace Blackfell who was deep in verse telling tales of old. Loosening his wolf skin cloak, Svenson turned his mind to the problem with which he had been wrestling for what seemed like an eternity. How was he to make his name? All of his great kinsman had gambled on the high seas, plundering foreigners for gold and silver. But this required a longboat, crew and all the trappings which would be needed for a rough and arduous voyage. He neither had the money nor the influence to bring together such a raiding party, and so something more extreme or cunning would have to be tried. But what?

Glowering now, with a hundred ribbons of shadow flickering across his chiselled face, Svenson looked up to Valhalla for inspiration. The heavy pine beams sturdily locked in place above seemed to bear down on him, trapping him in place. In desperation, he shifted his focus away to the first point of interest - an array of crafted metal work nailed onto the eaves. He recognised some of the designs on a breast plate, that of a mighty wolf who had conquered Odin and lead to Raganor; another sabre-hilt depicted a dragon perched upon a rocky outcrop, while a small shield bore the picture of a hideous water demon. He blinked, shook his head and marvelled at the idea that had begun to form. Svenson felt the ceiling recede into place as if a decision from the gods had been placed before him.

Turning to Blackfell, his mood improving with every second, he waited for his companion to finish his latest tale of murdered kings and bygone adventures. Blackfell had always been a lively entertainer and drew in his fellows with his wit and eloquent story telling. As Blackfell drew to a close, Svenson nudged him so violently he lurched forward and nearly fell off the bench. Pulling him back, his voice booming above the throng, Svenson thundered his intentions of slaying a monster so savage that all would hear the noise of the battle.

The laughter and banter died away from all quarters of the hall, while Svenson raised his massive body from his seat. He had done well; he had his audience. The tall Viking turned to face the crowd and said, "I hear there have been disturbances," holding his breath for a minute to maintain the suspense. "Randolph Garth in the next village has seen footprints so large that a fishing boat could be placed in each one. Thirty-foot pines have been uprooted and elk have been found half-eaten on the fell land to the south." The gathering throng circled around the giant man as if he were a piping-hot brazier on a frozen evening.

"Yes," he continued, "it is true. We have a lumbering monster in our midst. I believe it to be the Legend of Gothinn, a mighty troll." The words lingered in the air.

"A troll?" someone said from the crowd. "I thought a troll was a gigantic hog."

Another retorted that a troll was an old man who lived in the mountains, while yet another thought the troll was a cave dwelling reptile.

Svenson laughed and retorted, "Have you seen one, have you engaged in battle or seen a troll?"

The room went quiet and for a while all that could be heard were the winds outside and the swaying of the trees. Surveying the scene, Svenson was pleased at the silence that passed over the gathering. "And by Thor's own hammer, I will be the one to track and thwart the beast," yelled Svensen, forcibly banging on the bench. "Blackfell will tell you the legend of Gothinn," he said, staring at his compatriot for a second or two. Quizzically, Blackfell eyed his large acquaintance but then shrugged and stood up.

"The legend of Gothinn," Blackfell said, "is indeed long and almost lost as a legend, whispered only in secret at home when wine loosens the tongue. However, due to Gothinn's return, I must warn you of this mighty foe. He is said to stand the size of three men, standing one on top of another. The troll eats whatever meat he can get his hands on and will think nothing of dining on human flesh. He has long arms and legs with warty, bronzed skin and is the most repulsive creature you could imagine."

The crowd whispered in hushed voices before returning their worried eyes to Blackfell, who relished the attention. He told them more about the troll: he had acid breath that could paralyse his victims in minutes and the ability to heal himself rapidly from any wounds.

Svenson, now at the side of the hall and leaning against a wooden pillar, took over from Blackfell and remarked, "The only way to make sure the brute is dead is to subject his body to sunlight, which will instantly turn him to stone."

As the tale was told and retold around the settlement, and Randolph Garth reported the findings of Troll footprints to be true, the rumours began to escalate. It wasn't long before a bounty of gold was offered for the destruction of the troll, as long as proof could be given. More reports of troll trails were reported and several parts of animal bodies had been discovered in different remote locations.

One night, there was a terrific thunderstorm and the settlements of the Norsemen were battered and damaged. As everyone started to rebuild and make repairs, the news came from Lars Blue Tooth that Svenson the Red had slain Gothinn on the shores of Eccle, not ten miles from the settlement. Hasty provision was made to set sail and the company made their way across to the lonely beach.

As the longboat drew near, a figure on top of a pile of rock and rubble could be seen in the distance. The nearer the ship got, the larger the stone pile seemed. Svenson, covered in dirt, blood and sweat and holding an over-sized sledge hammer, acknowledged its presence.

"Did you hear the battle last night?" Svenson shouted, his torn, bloodied clothes hanging water-logged from his body. Ignoring the question, the important men of the settlement demanded to see the troll's body. Svenson laughed and said, "Can you not tell I am standing on top of the troll? We fought for hours before the dawn finally arrived. I drew him out to sea and, now, here Gothinn lies beaten to a stony pulp."

"But where is his body?" asked one. "I see only rocks!"

Svenson smiled. "Well, to make sure your troll is not coming back to life you have to dismember it, don't you? However, I saved a hand for you to admire." Pointing down to the base of the stones, they could indeed see the rough shape of a hand, clenched in a fist.

Blackfell looked on in admiration at scene - Svenson the Red mounted on a pile of stones and claiming a fortune for the privilege!

The House That Karl Built

Karl had built the modest dwelling with his bare hands. It was no small effort but he was fit and had the technical know-how. He remembered digging the foundations from the hard frozen ground, the wind whipping up around him as he toiled and sweated in the half light of winter. Sometimes the spade glistened when the sun deigned to show itself and he allowed himself a moment of pleasure in the new-felt warmth. His mind was fresh then, uncomplicated and unscarred by the weight of life. Energy was plentiful and surged through his body - life was good.

He had picked this spot as it seemed curiously wild compared to the little town in which he lived. Although only a few miles out, it seemed so quiet and rugged in comparison. On occasion, in the cold weather, he spotted pure white stoats weaving their way through the dry stone walls and often took joy in the lapwings' chaotic, looping flight. Glancing further afield, he marvelled at the copses, fells, marshy fields and unkempt uplands all knitted together like some outstanding undulating patchwork.

Karl recalled the coarse concrete that he had mixed in the spring, all those years ago. Bucket after heavy bucket blistered and cut his hands, until finally the base for the structure was level and solid. He had laid thick mortar and sandwiched it between bricks, speckled ash in colour. He had disregarded the local stone, opting for something new, something out of place, something *he* had chosen. His hands caked in mortar worked tirelessly and the sound of the scraping of the trowel on brick comforted him in the still, rural landscape. Time passed so rapidly, and every day a little progress was made. The walls began to take shape, strong and durable, well-crafted and satisfying to his eye. The beams of the structure were made from Scottish pine and the smell of the cut wood raised his spirits and added to the feeling of hard work and industry. He still remembered the joyous sound of the beams dropping into place with hollow thumps. As each rib was placed, he became more confident, and by the time he had set the last one, the skeleton of the house was completed.

Felt was unravelled over the beams and he had selected strange mottled green slate tiles from the Lake District to cover and protect the little cottage. Sitting on the roof, he hammered in sturdy long black nails with easy precision, feeling each smooth slate as it was positioned and attached. He lay on the concrete floor inside the building, looking up into the eaves of his creation, hearing the rattle of the rain pinging off the tiles. This is my own place he thought, feeling secure and well placed and as if nothing else mattered.

Once the remainder of the carpentry work and painting had been completed on the house, Karl remembered searching for new activities to fill his time. He piled up logs nearby; they were in plentiful supply and seemed to have been disregarded by local farmers. He rolled back one of the logs and started chipping away at it with hammer and chisel, peeling away the rough, wet exterior to reveal the dry fresh timber underneath. As he hammered and laboured, he had found that the process came naturally to him. In his mind he could envisage a magnificent woodpecker within the log and he warmed to the task of creating the image. He worked with the grain, dexterously carved feathers and beak, head and the bird's long tail. Surely but slowly, with every tap of the hammer, the bird took shape and within a week he had completely finished the creature. His work was seen in public and the detail and style of his work was commended. As a result, he was asked if it could be displayed in the local art gallery, to which he readily agreed.

Inspired by his almost instant success, Karl had beavered away obsessively creating sculpture after sculpture; a fox, weasel, owl, kite and wild cat soon followed, each with intricate detail. His work sold and he was able to make a living. Life was very good.

Karl stopped dreaming and his mind unwillingly came back into the present. Looking down at his chapped and worn fingers, he croaked bitterly as he climbed up to the ramshackle house he had once loved and cared for. There was no roof now and the walls were falling in.

Karl took a gasp from his oxygen mask and turned to his chubby carer to push him nearer. He shivered in the stiff wind and pulled his heavy winter coat tightly around him. The wheel chair moved sluggishly through the thick grass. Tears welled up in his eyes and he wheezed heavily. The house was barren and bare, given up to the elements and uncared for. Karl thought how time had passed so quickly back then, but now it seemed to drag. His time had passed and the end was fast approaching.

Jo Champney

Jo, who lives near Carlisle, has been a member of Carlisle Writers since 2011.

Elsa's Choice

"Granny! Granny! Are you there?"

Elsa Fraser, startled awake from her doze in the evening sun, smiled with pleasure at the sight of Neil, her grandson who was gallumping up the garden path. How tall he was growing, and how handsome with his red gold hair and clear blue eyes! More like his grandfather every day, but she had to remind herself not to hug and kiss him too much. He was ten next birthday, and no longer her little baby grandson, but he still gave her arm an affectionate squeeze as he flopped onto the swing seat next to her.

"Granny. Mum says if you tell me your six favourite numbers, she will put them on the lottery for you. What are they? Quick! Write them down. We're having this great game of football in the park!"

"Wait a moment now," said Elsa. "I can't just tell you something as important as that off the top of my head."

"Well, I know what the first one will be anyway," the boy laughed. "It has to be 10 because I'm ten on Friday, and that's my best number!"

"Look, Hedgie," she said, slipping back into the pet name she had called him when he was born and looked just like a spiky, twitchy-nosed hedgehog. "You go back to your game, and give me a little

45

more time to think this over."

"Right! I will be back when we've beaten them!" Neil called over his shoulder as he crashed down the garden path, through a lavender bush, through the garden gate which shuddered at his slam, and down the footpath to the playing field.

He may look like Peter but he certainly does not move like him, Elsa thought, relaxing again as the swing seat stopped shaking. Then, as she often did these days, Elsa slipped into a reverie, that blissful state between sleep and wakefulness where the past is clearer than this afternoon, and the years between them vanish in a gentle mist.

A seventeen year-old Elsa was walking with her mother in Argyle Street in the pouring rain. They were 'up town' as she recalled, to buy a present for her birthday, and there he was, walking just ahead of them in his officer's uniform, with the rain running in rivulets down his back.

It had been his walk, his graceful light-stepping walk, movement for all the world like a silver birch in a gale, strong-rooted but flexible, that had first drawn her eyes to him. The men she was used to wore boiler-suits and heavy tackety boots, and walked wearily back from the docks of an evening, or staggered angrily from the pubs and bars on a Saturday night. This man was so different. She was fascinated and watched as he turned, and in a soft lilting musical voice asked her mother the way to the Central Station.

Elsa moved a little on her seat and looked for a moment with pleasure at the garden; the containers of herbs on the patio where she sat, releasing their perfume into the soft evening air; the nasturtiums cascading from their hanging baskets, kaleidoscoping with the fiery geraniums and the fragrant lavenders. Then, as if drawn by an invisible cord, her mind swung back to the events of that amazing evening in August 1940.

Back, back…to her mother inviting him for tea, and this stranger who looked so at home sitting by the fire with her father, telling him about his childhood in Orkney, and his job in London where he had been assigned to 'special duties' because his skill in languages made him 'useful' in the 'cypher' section. He talked of his plans for 'when it was over', to teach in a university and spread his own joy in learning to all the youngsters who wanted to hear.

Elsa watched again her seventeen year-old self, washing dishes in the scullery with her mother, peeping through a crack in the door to hear the conversation that she felt too shy or ignorant to join in. She felt again her bewildering feelings of sadness and loss when Peter walked away from the house to station and out of her life forever.

As she lay sleepless in bed that night, she found herself crying over the impossibility of ever seeing him again. How could someone so clever and handsome with such an exciting and important job, meeting all those beautiful London women, ever give another thought to a Wee Glasgow Lassie who was out of school at fourteen and had not even heard of the languages he spoke.

But when the paths of kindred spirits cross, small miracles do sometimes happen, for as Elsa cried herself to sleep in her box bed, Peter, in the stuffy gloom of his southbound train, was wrapping, in a used envelope from his kit bag, a slim purple suede bound book of Shakespeare's sonnets, and addressing to Elsa to arrive in time for her birthday.

The days and weeks that followed passed in a daze. Work at the factory was hard and seemed harder when Elsa's section was moved out of the city and down to the country on the shores of the Solway. She remembered the ache of homesickness, and missed the closeness of her family and the friends she had grown up with.

Then the letters had started to arrive. Peter's letters were chatty and interesting, full of amusing details about life in London, and how he longed for the day when they would meet again. Elsa, who had never written anything in her life without anxiety, accompanied by the criticism of others, suddenly found herself looking forward to dinner breaks, not only for the relaxation, cigarettes and chat with her companions, but for the chance to take out her fountain pen, another of Peter's amazing presents, and the part-written letter, to spend a blissful fifteen minutes 'talking' on paper. She often opened the little book of poems and read one, feeling close to him in the shared joy of the beauty of words.

The ringing of the telephone called Elsa indoors, and a glance at the kitchen clock reminded her of Neil and the numbers. Now she had the first two, the rest would be easy. Her memory slipped effortlessly to June 20th 1946. Their wedding day had wiped away all the heartaches, anxieties and stresses of the war years and separation. She laughed out loud at the memory of herself on that day in her mother's wedding dress, made over to fit, shoes borrowed from a friend (how they had pinched!) and the posies of garden flowers, fetched up by a friend from Gretna, that filled the church with perfume.

The next few years blurred in Elsa's memory.

There was the excitement of Peter's first post at the university, and the demands which were put on her to meet and be at ease with so many new and important people. As always, his gentle encouragement boosted her confidence.

There was their first home, number twenty-one, the grey stone house that they had loved at first sight as they stood outside it together on an evening walk. It had looked so sad, empty and forlorn, with its broken window panes and overgrown garden, that they had longed to make it live again with light and laughter. Often in the days that followed, they walked past 'their' house and discussed what they would do; the painting and papering, the curtains and rugs, the garden with the digging and weeding, and the lavender bushes they would plant. They spent hours discussing the vital questions of where the considerable amount of money, probably the better part of a thousand pounds, could be found to buy the house and fulfil their dream, but no answer appeared.

The house remained in their hearts and minds until on a gentle evening in early September, the second of Elsa's miracles happened.

She had slipped out on her own to plant a tiny lavender cutting just inside the blue garden gate, for the hope of the future, she explained to herself, when an elderly lady with an ebony walking stick in one hand and a small dog on a lead in the other, called to her.

"Excuse me, my dear," she said.

Elsa jumped and brushing her knees in confusion mumbled, "I'm sorry, I didn't know. We thought it was empty. I am so sorry but..."

"Now I didn't mean to startle you," the old lady interrupted as she pushed open the garden gate and joined Elsa on the front path. "You see, the house is mine though it is empty. I don't live here now."

As Elsa began to turn away with another apology, a gentle hand on her sleeve made her pause.

"I live with my son and daughter-in-law just opposite. Won't you please come and have tea with me tomorrow, with your husband? It *is* your husband, isn't it?"

"Yes, yes. Peter is my husband," Elsa replied.

As if she feared that Elsa would disappear, the old lady hurriedly continued.

"You see, my dear, I have been watching you and your husband all these weeks, and it would make me so happy if you would live in this house. Perhaps if we could discuss a small rent, you would consider it?"

Of course, as Elsa was to tell her friends over the next few years, they did go to tea, they discussed a very small rent, they laughed and cried over the decorating and the gardening, and they found a special friend in whose company they delighted.

"Dear Mrs Seton," said Elsa aloud, rousing herself from her daydream. "Thank you, thank you for number twenty-one."

Elsa took a pencil from the terracotta pot on the sideboard and a note pad from the shelf at the window, and counted.

"I have ten for Hedgie, forty for the year I met Peter, twenty for our wedding day, twenty-one for our house. I need two more favourite numbers."

It was so restful just to sit at the big pine kitchen table in the evening sun, thought Elsa, but not like the earlier days when the house was never quiet and empty. It had always been busy, with students coming in for tutorials, dropping in for help and advice or just a mug of coffee with a chat that eased away the strangeness of being away from home for the first time. Girls in flared trousers and platform soles, boys with long hair and boots. All those boots. Elsa laughed at the recollection. She thought of all the young people walking through her life, but none of them her own children.

When they had first married, she had never thought of children. It had seemed to her they just happened along, everybody had them. Life was complete and perfect but, as the years rolled along, an aching gap began to open in the full and happy life at number twenty-one. Peter was busy doing what he loved and had always planned to do; teaching and passing on his love of languages with his passion for words and communication between people. But to Elsa, it seemed there was no way she could communicate with him on this one desperately unhappy area of her life. Her beloved husband had become a stranger.

She spent many sleepless nights, waking in the small hours of the morning, trying to think of ways to talk to Peter and explain how she felt, but she could find no answer to his habitual comment, "We have each other, don't we? Would a child make us any happier?" Elsa just knew in her heart it was what was needed to make them complete. She yearned to be a family, yet every attempt at conversation on the subject seemed to thicken the fog of misunderstanding that was building up between them.

"I'll soon be thirty-six," Elsa had said to a friend over coffee one morning. "It's hopeless. I'll never have a baby now."

She let loose a flood of tears that had been building up in the dark nights and empty spaces of days. When she had recovered and calmed enough to listen, the gentle question, "Have you ever thought of adopting?" came to Elsa like a gleaming golden shaft of sunlight that banished her darkness.

"Oh, Margaret!" she said. "Why didn't I think of that? I suppose I've been too busy feeling sorry for poor me. I just could not look outside myself. As soon as I can find a good moment, I will ask Peter if he will consider the idea."

"Oh, I need a cup of tea," said Elsa aloud to herself as she busied with the kettle and a dip into the biscuit barrel, recalling how often a cup of tea and a chat with Margaret had been a lifeline in the months of waiting that had followed their decision to try and adopt.

There were so many forms to be completed and interviews and inspections that, without her friend's willingness to be always there for her, Elsa could have easily slipped back into despair. Why was she even thinking of that time? Elsa shook herself and looked up instinctively to a photograph on the wall. Isabel, tiny, helpless and beautiful, had brought back the sunshine into their lives. She had been so small, born prematurely to a young mother who could not care for her, that she had been kept in hospital for three months. Three months of visits to 'their' baby, learning to bathe and care for this little scrap. How the nurses had laughingly reminded her, "She's not porcelain, you know!"

The day they brought her home, Elsa felt her happiness complete. She'd always known that looking after a new-born baby would be incredible, but she amazed herself at just how long she could sit by her pram under the shady tree in the garden, just watching her sleep. She never tired of leaning over the side of the cot with her finger grasped in her baby's sleeping fist, and Peter's arm around her shoulder. She particularly enjoyed early morning feeding times; at half past five in the morning, the outside world is quiet, and Elsa delighted in this special time by telling stories to her drowsy baby, stories that seemed to bubble up from a spring deep inside her, and wove a magic circle around the two of them.

It was on one of those mornings that Elsa was irritated to find that she felt vaguely unwell and decidedly queasy. "Oh, I have picked up a tummy bug!" she thought crossly. "I'll feel better tomorrow," but when she did not feel better on the four following mornings, a question began to form in her mind. The answer soon became obvious with a check of the calendar, but she still would not let herself believe that it was true.

Elsa looked at the other baby photographs on the sunlit wall. My two daughters, my two miracle gifts!

"I need one more number," mused Elsa, "just one more special number. Of course… it has to be my stories."

She selected a little book from four shiny dark green and gold volumes on the dresser. *The Dragonwell Stories.* She began to read and slowly turned over the pages, nodding now and then as if meeting an old friend.

"I never knew how much I wanted to write, it just happened!" she cried aloud.

"What just happened, Granny?" shouted Neil, as he rushed red-faced, muddy and excited into the kitchen. "What just happened?"

Elsa turned to greet him.

"Well, I was talking about my books, the stories I used to tell your mother and Aunt Isabel when they were small."

"Oh, yes," said Neil. "I've got them too. I liked them when I was young but now…"

His face puckered into a frown of disbelief as the kitchen clock struck eight.

"Now Mummy will be mad with me. She said to be home at seven, and to bring your numbers for the lottery. We were having such a cracking great game I just forgot. Sorry!"

Elsa gathered her grandson up in her arms for a brief hug.

"You go and wash your face while I give your Mum a call so she won't be worrying. Then we'll jump in the car, and have you home in five minutes."

As he pounded up the stairs, Elsa called over her shoulder, "Don't worry about the numbers, Neil. I've already had more joy from them than I could ever have had from a million lottery wins!"

Carpe Diem

Grieve not for me for I must die,

Better that you should know my warmth today

and feel the pressure of my arms.

Be grateful for your very need of me,

And pity other mortals who know not that urgency.

So hold me fast against the fleeting years,

And love me more for my mortality.

Overheard In An Old Churchyard

I wonder would you like to be, a knight upon a tomb with me?
Think you, my little hand would find a weakness in your armoury?

How many centuries of time would fly,
Before your stone-clad hand reached for my lichened thigh?
And we would be together, you and I.

Sarah Falder

Inspired to write by the countryside in which she grew up, Sarah enjoys sharing her work with the group. Born in Carlisle, Sarah grew up on both sides of the border and is currently studying for an Occupational Therapy B.Sc at the University of Cumbria.

Her eclectic hobbies include paranormal investigations, Viking re-enactments and playing bass guitar in a band. Her first love is, however, her writing.

Sanctuary

"Rest in peace, my beauties."

It was an automatic thought every time I passed the field. My four angels lay by the crumbling walls of the old barn. No one will ever know the magic of that old barn, hidden under collapsed stone walls and overgrown weeds, but for me it was my sanctuary.

The story of my childhood was never exhilarating; depressed and reserved northern English folk always kept to themselves, except for the purpose of whispering and gossip. His Lordship left my mother long before I left the womb, and yet she still gave me the bastard's name; a stigma that has always been with me. I wish she had abandoned me too. Maybe I would have had a chance in life. But no, the bitch dragged me down with her sinful ways, the alcohol and prostitution. As sinful as Mary Magdalene herself. I was more a burden than a convenience, only useful to be beaten to a pulp when things didn't go right. I could usually sense when something wasn't right, that's why I hid in the barn. If I could hide I wouldn't get hurt, but there are still plenty of scars to show from when I wasn't quick enough. In the end, I left her behind. The local church gave me work and a home, and embracing my faith, I took an oath to serve God. My missionary work took me all over the country until I was given a post running a refuge for vulnerable women. And that was my downfall.

For two years I watched victims walk through the door; guidance warmth and protection was all they ever desired. Drug users, victims of domestic abuse, all wanting to escape the hell they endured. Through rehabilitation and the love of God we helped them like a shepherd with his flock.

But there was always somebody who was too possessed to change. The devil resided in them and they soon slipped back into their old ways. Just like Jenny. She was the first, approaching the office late at night banging on my window. She was soaked from the storm raging outside. Of course, I let her in.

"You look ill," I said seeing her gaunt, pale features and dirty clothes hanging off her.

"I've just fallen on hard times," she said looking at me, "but I need help. Will you help me?" I pulled out the necessary papers and discussed with her the things we could do to help her.

"No," she said, "I just need money." The desperate tone in her voice cut me to the quick. It the same tone my mother would use when she needed another drink. It was the same every time.

"I'm not giving you money, Jenny." I said calmly. "I can help you with your problems but you have to cooperate."

"Just a few quid will get me back on my feet," she pleaded. "You'll see, I can change. I just..."

"No, Jenny," I said firmly.

She clasped her hands around her head in frustration. She ran to the desk throwing open the drawers.

"Jenny! Stop!" I shouted, trying to grab her.

"No! I need money! I thought you were supposed to help me."

I tried pulling her away but she turned around and slapped me. That's when I lost it. I grabbed her throat. My hatred and loathing of women who abused themselves had come to the surface. After all I had done to help her and all she could do was slap me! Within a moment she had flopped to the floor. I had killed her.

I didn't panic. I could see a path I hadn't expected present itself to me. I picked the body up effortlessly, carrying it out the back door to my car in the wet darkness. Sliding Jenny's body into the boot, I drove mechanically out of the town. There was only one place set clearly in my mind - my sanctuary.

Shovel in hand, I dug under the broken tree. It took hours, wet soil piling up in the dark and the hole quickly filling with water. There was a gentle splash as I tossed the body in. Grief and guilt should have consumed me but instead I had an epiphany. That night, I had saved Jenny from the devil and from herself. I had given her up to God for safe-keeping and repentance.

And there in my secret sanctuary, Jenny lies with all the others I have saved. No doubt more will join her...

Transition

The last breath has escaped.
I see a familiar face.
A sense of calm comes over me,
As I welcome death's embrace.

My entity rises above.
I look below and see myself,
No longer a solid being,
I drift away with stealth.

The mourners begin to arrive,
Weeping tears for my loss.
But they do not realise I'm here,
Hoping they won't make a fuss.

They give me a traditional goodbye,
A ritualistic farewell.
The light above me pulls me up,
I realise I won't go to hell.

I land in a world of paradise,
With sunshine and clear blue skies.
I see others, who left before me,
And greet them with joyous cries.

Now I am settled in heaven,
An eternal life of dreams.
Even my darkest memory,
Shows golden as it gleams.

Work In Progress

The street had been silent until a removal van pulled in, its tyres rumbling over the cobbles until it screeched to a halt outside one of the many terraced houses lined along the street. The doors of the van opened and two men jumped out, making their way towards the back, opening up the hatch. A woman stepped down from the passenger side of the van, lighting up a cigarette. Her face was pale, a bleak grey skin tone matching the walls of the house she stared up at. She walked towards the red door from which paint had flaked off leaving bare patches of wood. Her hand was shaking as she turned the key in the lock. As the door creaked open, she stared into the hallway ahead of her and she thought to herself, "Welcome home, Jenny."

She left the front door wide open and shut herself in the kitchen at the back of the house. She took another long drag from her cigarette as she listened to the removal men placing her meagre possessions into the living room as they had been instructed. She busied herself with an imaginary to-do list, thinking about the most important things she needed to sort out. Top of the list was internet access; with that she wouldn't need to worry about unwanted human contact. Social anxiety had always been a problem for Jenny; in twenty years she had rarely left the confines of the house, only interacting with her parents, her tutor, the maid and the doctor. Everything might be different now; moving house was just the first challenge.

The removal men left after half an hour. Most the furniture was in the front room; she carried what she could upstairs to the bedroom. Suddenly, there was a knock at the door. Jenny froze. She wasn't expecting visitors. No one she'd arrived.

Another knock. A voice called through the letter-box: "Hello? I'm Margaret from number 23. Just want to welcome you to the street." Jenny hid behind the door until she heard the flap bang shut. She breathed a sigh of relief when it was silent again and tiptoed back down to the living room, where she made sure the blinds were tightly closed. She set up her laptop and ordered a takeaway over the internet. She thought to herself that she would have to get in some proper food supplies tomorrow, along with a fridge and cooker.

Twenty minutes later, there was a banging on the door.

"Who is it?" she whispered.

"Pizza delivery! I have your double pepperoni," a voice replied.

"Just leave it on the doorstep," she said, almost pleading.

"Are you sure? There's already something on the step," he said.

Jenny pushed some loose change through the letter-box, hoping a tip would make the boy leave. It seemed to do the trick as she heard the car driving away. She opened the door quickly, grabbing the pizza box and the object that was underneath. She placed the pizza on her lap and put the other object onto the table; it was an old Quality Street sweet tin. She opened the lid to find a freshly-made lemon drizzle cake. The smell assailed her nostrils and her mouth watered. She immediately replaced the lid as tears began to flow. Lemon cakes had always been her favourite. She had never smelt one as good as this since she left home. "This is my home now - a new chapter in my life," she thought to herself as she started eating her pizza.

"The last two days have been a nightmare," Jenny said, sitting on her living room floor, with her arms wrapped around her knees. Dr James, her therapist, was sitting on the only chair looking down at her.

"We knew it was going to be a difficult and a slow process, Jenny. You just need to take it a day at a time. You're doing splendidly so far," he smiled, taking off his glasses and wiping them clean before putting them back on. "I can't give you any more medication and it's no good using it to hide from your problems. You will need to get used to it."

"I know. It's just so hard and people are so intrusive," Jenny replied, remembering how her neighbour, Margaret, had been at her door on no fewer than five occasions. The last time she had even resorted to banging on the living room window.

"Have you sorted yourself with food and other necessities? I see you ordered some furniture," he said, referring to the flat-pack Ikea boxes piled up in the corner.

"Yes, I found something called Tesco's home delivery. They brought it to my door yesterday after the fridge and the washing machine arrived," she answered.

"And how did you cope?" Dr James asked.

"I let the man in with the fridge and the washer, and I hid upstairs smoking half a packet of cigarettes during the hour while he was here. I wanted to scream for him to leave when he came up looking for the toilet."

"And how did you respond?" he asked again.

"I told him to go outside to pee... and to bang the door when he left."

Dr James chuckled at her response. "Well, you used some initiative! I'm sorry, Jenny," he said, "but I really must be going. I will come back next week at the same time and see how you're doing. If you need me, just ring the surgery or e-mail me." He let himself out the front door.

"Instructions are always useless..." Jenny remembered her dad saying, when he was fixing parts of his car; now here she was attempting to assemble flat-packed furniture. She looked again in frustration at the instructions. She had only just managed to fix up a small bedside cabinet but this chest of drawers was a different kettle of fish. Her fingers scrambled around the screws, feeling for the screwdriver and she attempted for the third time to screw in the bolt and hold the two pieces together. The upright side fell down again for the third time and clattered onto the concrete yard floor. Jenny growled in irritation, throwing the screwdriver down.

"Do you need a hand?"

A male voice from behind shocked her. She turned around to see the most unusual looking man her; she took one glance at him and ran into the house. Taking deep breaths, she reached for her cigarette packet, found it empty and threw it across the room in anger. She sank down against the wall sobbing, knowing she had to face the world and not be afraid of it. Jenny managed to calm down and control her breathing. Eventually, she stood up and opened the door. It must have taken longer than she realised to compose herself as, when she opened the door, she saw an assembled chest of drawers with the screwdriver sitting on top. There was no-one there, so she calmly stepped out to manoeuvre the drawers back into the building.

Her mind had raced for hours about the incident, but after much analysing, she decided she would be brave enough to acknowledge the stranger. She kept watching out of the kitchen window, waiting for the stranger to return; she also left the back door slightly ajar so if anyone was outside she would hear them. In the end it came to nothing; she saw no-one throughout the day.

It was the same again the next morning except for Margaret banging on her door and window yet again. This time, however, Jenny felt brave enough to stick her hand through the blinds and made an unfriendly gesture. By lunchtime, she had given up waiting for him. She spent the afternoon watching cookery programmes, and looking at recipes; she needed a better diet as the most experimental thing that she'd ever prepared was a cheese and ham sandwich. After the programme finished, Jenny felt confident enough to try out a new recipe. She also wanted to use the new frying pan that she'd had ordered from the shopping channel on TV. It looked simple enough to begin with; the bacon and vegetables were cooking in white wine. They were sizzling away on the hob when the white wine sauce ignited. She turned the ring off and moved the pan from the heat. The bacon and juice sizzled even more loudly. Jenny didn't want to set off any alarms so she did the only thing she could think of and took the smoking pan outside to the back yard. She was cautiously trying to set it on the ground when something hot spat out of the pan and landed on her exposed arm.

She cried in pain, grasping her arm and letting the pan drop to the ground. She didn't realise when someone grabbed her other arm and took her back into the house. In a blur of searing pain she heard a voice saying, "Are you okay? What happened?" She found herself looking at the neighbour who had fixed her chest of drawers. He held her scalded hand firmly under the cold tap.

The only sound in the room was the trickling of the water.

"My name's Mark," he said, breaking the silence.

Jenny's mouth had gone dry; she was too overwhelmed to respond immediately. She moistened her lips and replied "I'm Jenny."

"Do you have a first aid kit, Jenny?" he asked. Jenny shook her head. He let go of her arm and moved towards the door.

"Keep your arm under the tap. I'll be right back," he said.

Mark returned a few minutes later with an old biscuit box. "You can turn the tap off now. It should be enough," he said as he opened the box and took out a sterilized gauze pad. He walked towards her, gesturing for her to hold out her arm. She held it up and he carefully placing the gauze on the burn and sticking it in place with surgical tape.

"Thank you," Jenny said when he was done. Mark smiled and turned towards the door, picking up his box. "Don't go!" she pleaded. He turned back to her. "Thank you for putting the flat-pack together, and... " she held up her arm, smiling. "I'm sorry that I'm not good with other people around," she said.

"I know," he answered. "Dr James used to be my therapist too a few years back. I saw him leave the other day. I also found your plumber urinating against my wall!"

Jenny laughed, "I am sorry!" she said. "Why did you see Dr James?"

"I was in the army a few years back as a medic. I was shot though," he answered, lifting his T-shirt to show a rather ugly scar on the side of his stomach. "Let's just say I needed a lot of therapy to forget the horrors I saw."

Jenny spoke up. "My dad worked in the embassy. He was assassinated when I was nine. After that, my mother never left our house and wouldn't let me either. She died of cancer last year."

"I'm sorry for your loss," he said.

"It's okay. My mum made a will to sell our house and money was put in trust so I had some income. All the furniture was sold too."

"Well, you haven't run away from me screaming this time," he

67

said smiling.

"I'm sorry. I've never seen someone with hair like the plume on a Roman soldier's helmet! Nor with a bolt through their nose!"

Mark burst into laughter. "This hairstyle is a Mohican," he said. "My bolt is called a septum piercing; it's similar to a bullring, I'm a Taurus you see."

"Oh," was all Jenny could say, rather embarrassed. "Would you like to stay for dinner?" she asked him.

"Sure. I think your bacon is ruined though," he answered. "I'm not much of a cook but I can order a pizza."

"If you'll answer the door." she said.

"Sure, sounds like a plan. By the way, did you enjoy the lemon cake?" he asked.

"How did you know about that?" she replied.

He smirked. "I made it myself. I left it for you after I heard nosey Margaret at your door."

"Well, I will tell you all about that while we eat," Jenny laughed. And for the first time in her life she entertained a new friend.

Alfa Bennett

Alfa joined Carlisle Writers in 2000; the invaluable support and encouragement of other group members has helped her move forward with her writing.

Alfa has been creating stories and poetry since her school days, where she was encouraged by inspirational teachers. Working with children and writing stories for her own family ensured she kept on writing over the years.

Twisted Fate

From a very early age, Mickey McManus was an opportunist and potential conman. With his black curly hair and cheeky impudent smile, he certainly knew how to milk the market as few could resist his appealing ways.

It was Mickey, a budding entrepreneur at eight years of age, who worked out that every fifth coin that went in made the bubble gum machine throw out two packers instead of the usual one. He hovered in close proximity to the machine until four hopefuls had put in their coins, then inserted his own five pence coin and got his free packet of gum. A fine profit. At weekends, he was known to spend several hours by the machine. This was the start of his many ingenious scams.

By the time he left school, Mickey had amassed a sizeable bank account and having acquired, in the face of strong competition, a job as a trainee mechanic in a back street garage, life was treating him well. He was soon doing 'foreigners' on the side (an ambiguous but nonetheless true statement.) Mickey learned how to cut corners and, judging by the state of some of the cars that left the garage, get away with murder. And all the while his bank balance was growing.

When the garage owner was treated to a long holiday at Her Majesty's pleasure for malpractice, Mickey grabbed the opportunity to buy the run-down garage. His Midas touch did not let him down, and only a year later he sold the land and premises to a supermarket chain for an obscene amount of money. His cultivation of one of the directors had paid off, as he knew it would.

One would think that Mickey would now rest on his laurels and enjoy his wealth, but cons and scams were in his blood; they were what fed his adrenalin and gave him zest for life. He spent the next five years acquiring and opening up small garages in the most remote and isolated parts of Britain, the idea being to have a monopoly, charge exorbitant prices and do a makeshift job on repairs. In many cases, cars went in and came out in the same precarious state. Mickey's Motors mechanics knew the score.

But this was not the case with Highcliffe, a relatively new garage in the Mickey's Motors chain. It was the highest garage in England, nestling into the Pennine chain, with access gained by a winding road with hairpin bends and severe drops. Highcliffe's inhabitants and nearby isolated sheep farmers were still in ignorance about the non-service which Mickey offered them.

Once a month, Mickey personally drove round in his red Lexus collecting the takings from each remote garage. Just when customers were beginning to ask questions, he would close down and do a moonlight flit. A shout and they were gone.

Mickey had spent the day counting money and checking books, and he began driving his way down to the hotel, anticipating a hot bath, good food and congenial company, when the engine spluttered and cut out. He limped over to a passing place and parked up. True to form, his luck was in, as within minutes an open-backed farm truck pulled in behind him and the driver got out. After phoning Mickey's Motors on his mobile to collect the Lexus, he accepted the farmer's offer of a lift down into the town. The truck pulled out and the two men exchanged pleasantries.

"It's lucky you came along. I could have been there for hours," said Mickey.

"Aye, lad, you're right. But lucky it wasn't yesterday it happened," the farmer replied, as the truck gathered momentum and negotiated the next hairpin bend on the rough, twisting road.

"Oh? Why?" asked Mickey, clinging to the front dashboard.

"Oh, truck was in the garage. Losing brake fluid, and the brake cable was nearly worn through. A death trap by all accounts, but the garage fixed it real quick. I just picked it up half an hour ago."

The words penetrated Mickey's brain and he had just time, before the truck gathered further speed, hit a hairpin bend above a tremendous drop and careered over the side, to utter a shout. And they were gone, turning and twisting all the way down.

71

Life's Cycle

A wizened, decaying apple, clinging by a thread, isolated on the now barren, naked tree.

The same tree which once, not long ago, stood tall like an Indian prince, bedecked in robes of shimmering reds, oranges and gold.

The hard ground is wearing its armour of snow as the apple falls, sinking down into the downy whiteness, to wait for its resurrection to new life as the seeds escape the rotting flesh to be consumed by the earth.

They lie dormant till youthful Spring, clothed all in green, paints on the trees young delicate shoots and buds that glisten in the mist as the pale watery sun breaks through. As the buds unfurl and fan out, spreading over the branches, new life emerges everywhere.

Summer, calm and serene, covers the branches with blossom of every hue - white, pink, cerise and red, and soon tall, blossomed trees sway in the breeze like dancers at a ball.

The blossom fades away, and the small hard fruit appears, at first unnoticed but growing, expanding, until the shiny ripe fruit is abundant, peeping out from amongst the already red, orange and golden leaves.

Winter comes like a hunter, with eyes like stone; the leaves curl, the fruit falls. Winter has made its kill and only…

A wizened, decaying apple is clinging, by a thread, on the now barren naked tree.

When Green And Beige Make Red

When the plane doors opened and I stood on the steps, the rancid, pungent smell of rotting, putrefying vegetation and the claustrophobic, humid temperature engulfed me. I looked down from that great height onto the multiracial, multicultural, multi-religious indigenous peoples of this island, people whom I would live amongst and grow to know so well. I could hardly believe that I, at twenty-two and the personification of innocence and naivety, had left my small picturesque Cumberland village nine thousand miles behind me.

Singapore was a city of contrasts. Skyscrapers towering above wooden shacks; wide tiled boulevards feeding nervous, twisting, heaving smoky streets. Mercedes cars running smoothly along, while rickshaws and trishaws were pulled and propelled by barefooted boys, weaving in and out of rush hour traffic. Smart sophisticated brief-cased commuters rubbing shoulders with pyjama-clad, coolie-hatted Chinese basket carriers. Dalston was far away, becoming a fading dream.

A month later, having found a house, a lovely spacious bungalow on the Malayan peninsula, I started my job at St John's Army Senior Comprehensive School at Tanglin Army Base, the setting for *The Virgin Soldiers* film. I felt confident and acclimatised. Even the mosquitoes were losing interest in my fast-thinning blood. My face was now pale brown, and the overheated crimson red of the last month had gone forever. Or so I thought…

The confrontation between Indonesia and Malaysia necessitated the presence of British armed forces in large numbers as Indonesian infiltrators came over the Jahore Straits in sanpans. *The Straits Times Journal* was full of stories of atrocities and gave dire warnings to be on guard against the enemy. Very worrying to a simple country girl whose biggest danger had been to get across Scott's Field during the mushroom season without being noticed by the bull!

Green and beige made red. You want to know how? Even now, all these years later, my pulse pounds when I think about it....

St John's School was twenty miles from my bungalow, which involved my taking the Naval School bus each day, manned by an Indian, Malay or Chinese driver. We crossed the causeway separating the island and the mainland, took the dual carriageway and then turned off at Bukka Timar village, following the narrow road up through the jungle to Tanglin Army Camp. The children on the bus ranged in age from fourteen to twenty year-old sixth formers, not much younger than myself!

Hitherto, each day's journey had proved uneventful, the only deviation being when our Indian driver occasionally stopped the bus to pick poppies for his opium pipe! On this particular day when we left the main road, little did I know what terror lay ahead.

I was dozing like Sleeping Beauty in the jungle (well, it was 7am!) when the bus suddenly stopped. All around us was an ominous silence. Our driver was a diminutive Malay without any English. Children looked at each other, children looked at teacher, teacher looked at driver, who was now gesticulating towards the road outside. Stretched across the road in front of us, I could see a line of green and beige uniforms, dark faces, bits of foliage stuck in metal helmets, and guns with bayonets drawn, pointing at the bus!

Positioned now behind the driver, I could not think, I could not speak and I could not move, frozen like Lot's wife into a pillar of salt. The children were huddled together at the back of the bus like figures in an Impressionist painting until Polly Rice pleaded, "Do something, Miss!" What the hell did she expect me to do? Armed combat? I'd missed out on lessons for that at the Carlisle and County High School!

An officious individual, small in stature, detached himself from the line, and pounded on the bus door, indicating that our driver should open it. Putting a restraining hand on his shoulder, I shook my head. I felt a soft touch from behind me, and turned to see Henry, the senior prefect, had joined me.

"Let's sit it out!" he said.

So there we were; a typical country lass and a slightly built sixth-former facing six, armed Indonesian infiltrators. It was a stand-off. Time stood still. We waited. After much banging, shouting, and then conferring with each other, the line of men parted and faded off into the jungle, soon hardly visible because of the green and beige camouflaged uniforms.

Drive! That was enough. The bus moved forward, and you could feel the passengers' iron bands of tension slacken. We had done it, we were free, we had survived! After a mile, we were picked up by a British Military Police escort which followed our bus at a discreet distance, the soldiers' red caps reassuringly visible. But… where were they when we had needed them?

Soon we were on Tanglin Road, and turning into Dover Road. The school loomed up and we turned into the long inclined drive. I was shaking with relief. We swept round the fountain, and then I saw them; army big brass, officers, military police, and the head and deputy head of the school. The bus circled and stopped. The head and a colonel appeared at the door of the bus.

"Are you OK? Can you leave the bus?"

But it was not a request, it was a question! "Stupid, strange question!" I thought. And then came his next words.

"We had a red alert. Our Gurkha jungle patrol radioed in to say that when they routinely stopped your bus, you would not or could not open the door. They feared that infiltrators had boarded the vehicle, preventing you from opening the door."

I just wanted to die! Green and beige camouflage uniforms - Gurkhas, revered soldiers of the British Army and I hadn't known! I felt the heat first, then the colour came, my neck suffused with pink which spread to my face that eventually turned scarlet.

So that's how the green and beige made red. Innocence and naivety personified! You can take the girl out of Dalston, but never Dalston out of the girl.

And recently, I added my support to Joanna Lumley's campaign to grant British citizenship to Gurkhas. I felt I owed it to them!

Brenda Hunter

Brenda enjoys writing and has been a member of the writers' group since 2000.

Brenda grew up on the Raffles estate in Carlisle and often draws on the people she knew there for her stories. She has three children, two sons and a daughter, as well as several grandchildren. She is a retired SEN nurse.

Leaving Paul

Tina and Paul had been staying with their friend Tim in London, but they had to leave as Tim was behind with his rent and was moving back to his parents' house.

Tina was fed up with Paul and was thinking of a way to leave him. Last time she left him, he came to her mother's house in Edinburgh and, against her mother's advice, she returned home with him. She just didn't want to hear her mother say, "I told you so." She had felt trapped with Paul now and he was spending all her money. She had a good job in the Council Office and had helped Tim with the rent, but the last payment had gone missing and Tina suspected Paul of taking it, probably for his drugs or gambling.

They rowed over money a lot, with Paul not working. Every time she saved up some money, Paul had needed it. Lately, Paul had been meeting her after work, and made her let him use her bank card for ready cash. She felt trapped. She had had enough, and had made up her mind she was leaving him.

And now seemed to be the right time! She got a lovely post card from her mother with fancy lettering saying 'Scotland' showing a stag standing by a loch. This reminded her of home in Edinburgh. On the card which Tina sent to her mother, she had instructed her not to phone her mobile, as Paul checked it and had lately been violent with her. She didn't tell her mother that on the card but she would when she was home. She hoped her plan would work and soon she would be on the train northwards for home.

That evening, Tina hid fifty pounds inside an Ordnance Survey map of Pitlochry for her friend Tim. She had told Tim she would pay his train fare home to his parents, and how she would give him the money secretly, because Paul didn't miss a thing. She knew that Paul would be angry, so she just said, "Here is the map you wanted, Tim." Tim smiled and took it. The trick went unnoticed by Paul.

Tina had confided in a friend at work. She took her to see the boss, who was very helpful. She even went with her to the bank, and advised Tina to transfer her money into another account.

It only left Tina with fourteen pounds in her account with no overdraft facility, so if Paul attempted to use her card that would be all the money he could get. Wary of him, she carefully hid the cash in different places. Tina was not leaving anything to chance. The new account card would be sent to Tina's mother's house. At twenty-five, Tina was able to support herself. She was so pleased she hadn't married him. More good advice from her mother!

She was all packed, filling two suit cases, and these she took to the station to be sent on ahead to Edinburgh. Everything was done while Paul was out seeing someone about where they would live tomorrow, now that Tim could not have them. All Tina had to do was pick up the last of her belongings and say goodbye to Tim who had been a good friend. She had no wish to see Paul.

"I am going now, Tim, before Paul gets back. Here is my mother's address. I will keep in touch. I am sure Paul stole your £700 rent money," she added. "It wasn't me."

"I know it wasn't you, Tina. I've caught Paul stealing before."

Paul didn't often leave them alone to talk, as he was a jealous man. This was a rare time with him out. He usually saw his friends during the day when Tim and Tina were both at work. Tina picked up her bag and was leaving when Paul suddenly appeared.

"I have sorted us a few nights to stay over at Mick's place. Hey! Why have you got your coat on? What's going on?"

Tina said, "Goodbye, Paul. I am going to stay with a girl from work. I am not living like this."

Paul grabbed her and said "You're going nowhere without me!" and he slapped her face.

Tim said, "Don't you hit her!" as he took her hand and helped her up.

Tina had lost her balance and had fallen down by the cupboard, cutting her head on the brass handle of the cupboard door.

Paul said "Don't you blame me for that blood. I only gave you a slap,"

"You are terrible, Paul," said Tim. "You shouldn't hit her at all. You don't deserve a girl like her."

"And you do, I suppose?"

"I don't want Tim," gasped Tina. "I have a place to live with a girl-friend. I'm going right now and I don't want to see you again, Paul. We are over!"

"You don't mean that!" Paul shouted, and went to stop her from leaving but Tim grabbed him and held him till Tina got out.

She tried to run but felt dizzy so walked slowly down the street, glad to have only one bag and her hand bag, and so pleased to have sent the cases on. Tina hoped Tim would be all right. Three times before she had left Paul and he had always managed to talk her round, but this time she knew he couldn't. Her face felt wet and she stopped and took out her handkerchief. She found that the blood from her head was running down it. Then she heard footsteps and Paul was almost beside her.

"Don't be silly, Tina. We can go to Mike's," he said as he grabbed at her arm.

"I don't want you anymore. I am sick of you. Let me go!"

Two policemen were talking to a woman nearby. Tina called for help and they both ran over to her. The blood from her head wound was trickling down her face. She wiped it again with her handkerchief.

"Please keep him away from me, please" she begged them, and then she passed out.

When Tina came to she was in the police car on her way to hospital. She still had her bags with her and Paul was not there, so she relaxed. Tina told the female police officer who was dabbing her head with a clean handkerchief what had happened, and the officer went into the hospital with her. She had four stitches put in her head, and was given a letter for her doctor, instructing her what to do for the next few days.

Then the officer took her to the police station and took down the full story. They were going to charge Paul with assault, but Tina explained he'd have left Tim's flat by now and she had no knowledge of Paul's new address as they had split up.

All she only wanted to go home to Scotland to her mother. They took Paul's mobile number from Tina as well as her mother's address, and she phoned a taxi to take her to the railway station. The officer told her to be careful and she left. When she was on the train, Tina phoned her mother and told her she had missed the intended train, but would be on the next one. Her mother said, "Your father and I will meet you." She felt relieved.

As she sat on the train, the steward came with the food trolley. Tina asked for a cup of black coffee and a sandwich. She sat drinking and feeling relaxed at last, enjoying the peace. Checking her purse and ticket she saw two Scottish five pound notes that her mother gave her on her last visit, one from the Clydesdale Bank, the other from the Royal Bank of Scotland.

The banknote with picture of a bridge over a burn reminded Tina of her favourite film, *Brigadoon*. A love story. But the star of the film was not someone like Paul, who needed more and more money lately. She realised now that she had been afraid of Paul, and had wasted six years of her life with him with nothing to show for it.

As the train sped north, Tina realised that she had left that old life behind, and that she was making a fresh start. Paul was in the past, and she was escaping into the future. Tina snuggled into her seat with a contented sigh. From now on, life was going to be good!

Irene

Irene waddled into the hotel, feeling that she had made the right decision about what she had to do in there, but she did not want anything to go wrong. It was a posh hotel, to which she had been many times, so that she knew her way to the large function area called the Swiss Room.

As Irene walked into the middle of the function room, she raised her voice above the chatter and said, "Is this the Fat Class?" The voices continued, but a small lady came over to Irene and said kindly, "No, dear. This isn't a class, it is a private function." The lady took Irene by the hand, and gently pulled her away from the centre of the room.

"My name's Mary. What's yours?"

Irene didn't want to say her name, and stayed silent.

"Don't be embarrassed, dear," smiled Mary. "I used to go to a fat class. I don't think you can stay in this room. You had better leave."

"Thank you for bothering to help me," said Irene.

Irene realised that a lot of people were staring at her. She looked down at her fat body, with the tight zip jacket and the cheap coloured trainers on her feet. She chuckled to herself. Her hair and make-up were perfect, but the tight shorts were uncomfortable. She did not like being fat!

She moved around the room, carefully noticing all the people were wearing name tags. She talked for a while to Linda. A little man with a moustache had his name tag, 'John', upside down, and when Irene pointed this out, he was very rude and told her to leave the room because she shouldn't be there. When Irene said, "You are very rude. It costs nothing to be nice," he left her abruptly and crossed the room to talk to somebody else. Irene watched him, and wrote in a little note book that she had taken from her back pocket.

Suddenly a tall man approached her, and asked her to leave in a very abusive manner. He had no name tag, and Irene asked him who he was.

"I'm Michael Smith, and I am throwing you out!"

He grabbed her arm and pushed her out of the door. Irene waited a little while, then returned to the room, mingling with the crowd. She avoided the unpleasant men, and she did not mind that they would be talking about her. In the next few minutes, Irene spoke to several people; some were pleasant, some were not.

A lady called Susan stood up and clapped her hands.

"I am told that the food is ready, so you may go through to the dining room."

When everyone was seated, Irene walked into the room but was physically stopped by two men. They each took a wrist and dragged her from the room. She fell awkwardly but they continued to drag her. They began to swear at her and be abusive, but she did not retaliate as they pushed her out of the door.

Mary appeared and said, "I am very sorry, my dear. They should not have done that to you!"

"Thank you for your concern," said Irene, "but please go back into the meal."

As Mary left her, she smiled and said, "I hope you find your class!"

Irene waited a few minutes, and was joined by another lady, Mrs Campbell whom all the diners knew from work. The two of them walked into the seated gathering, and one of the bullies who had thrown her out shouted, "Don't bring that fat cow back in here!"

"I am afraid that I must," said Mrs Campbell, "because this is your new boss!"

His face went red, and the muttering in the room died down to silence. Irene went to the top table and spoke.

"I am Irene Shaw, your new manager, and if you would just wait a minute..."

In front of them all, Irene unzipped her jacket and removed it along with all the padding from a body suit, and the ugly trainers. Underneath the padding was a small woman, size twelve, clad in a smart black dress. She slipped on her black shoes.

"Let me explain. I was disguised by a friend I have who works in films. I wanted to meet you while you were unaware of whom I was, to see how you react to a person." Waving her notebook in the air, Irene continued, "Some of you are awful, and I want changes!" She put her notebook on the table, and spoke.

"A lot of you will be demoted. I have made notes tonight, and some of you just do not have the right attitude for this job. We work with people in every walk of life but some of you are very judgemental and have no empathy for other people. You watched me go around this room tonight, and some of you were very kind. When we work with other people, I insist you treat them the way you would like to be treated yourselves. All those people who come into our office, they have their dignity."

Irene then nodded to the head waiter who told his staff to start serving.

"Enjoy your meal," said Irene, "and we have this time to bond and get to know each other. I hope to send you home better people, and when on Monday our office doors open, you will all be more helpful…. at the DSS. Now, eat!"

They all ate in silence.

The Swing Of The Pendulum

The old clock stood proud in the auction room. There were a lot of people interested in it. Amy hoped they would bid on anything but the clock. She had set her heart on it but she wanted it for less than its thousand pound reserve. The picture on its face was of a country scene that reminded Amy of a place she had visited when she was very young. She had a suspicion too it had once belonged to her grandmother. The small mark on its side seemed to confirm it was the same clock her grandmother had owned.

Amy was with friend her friend Ann who had never been to an auction before. Amy told her not even to scratch her nose in case the auctioneer thought she was bidding and she ended up accidentally buying something. Eventually the noise in the room died down and the bidding began. The auctioneer started at one thousand and fifty pounds for the clock. From there it went beyond the amount Amy could afford. It was sold to small man for one thousand, five hundred pounds. Amy was so disappointed but she and Ann stayed a little bit longer.

Ann was very pleased with the pink and green tea-set she bought for twenty pounds as well as several other items. Amy herself bought 'a large wooden box with contents' that cost her ninety-nine pounds. It had a picture carved on the top and the key to its metal lock was given to Amy when she paid. They loaded up the car with their purchases and drove home.

Once inside the house, the friends looked at the carving on the box, and Amy suddenly realised that it was identical to the one on the face of the clock that she had wanted to buy. Her face lit up with a big smile as she opened the box and she remembered that her grandmother had one just like it. There was a secret compartment, she recalled, which she managed to release. Inside there were some papers and a few coins in a small tin box as well as a beautiful silver pen with a purple stone at the top. She knew instantly it *was* her grandmother's special box and when she found a photograph of her grandmother and herself as a girl, it confirmed everything for her. Amy searched further. She spotted a brown paper bag in the corner of the secret compartment. Inside it was a well-made, small brass clock carved with intricate figures and several old-fashioned five-pound notes.

The two girls looked at each other and laughed. Finally, underneath everything else, there was a cloth bag. Inside was a brass pendulum.

"I bet that belongs to a grandfather clock," said Ann.

Suddenly, the phone rang. It was the man from the auction room.

"Excuse me, Mrs Loveday," he said, "I'm Roy from the auction room. Did you find a pendulum in the box you bought today?"

"Yes," Amy said, hesitantly.

"It would seem that it's the pendulum for the grandfather clock that we sold today. Unfortunately, the purchaser won't complete the sale unless the pendulum is in place."

"I'm sorry," Amy retorted, "but that's hardly my fault. I bought the box and its contents in good faith. It's your problem."

"I'll offer you fifty pounds for it," the man said.

"Definitely not," Amy snapped. "The pendulum is not for sale. Unless, of course, you increase your offer." And she put the phone down.

Ann giggled. "You drive a hard bargain," she said.

Later that day, Roy arrived at Amy's house. He told her that the sale for the grandfather clock had fallen through because the pendulum was missing. He offered her the clock at the reduced price of eight hundred pound, which turned out be within her original budget. Amy gleefully accepted.

Amy and Ann fitted the pendulum to the old grandfather clock. It fitted perfectly and chimed well. As soon as it began to tick, childhood memories flooded over Amy.

She couldn't wait to tell her mother about buying her grandmother's box. Her mother was amazed to hear about the secret compartment.

"Well, you've done very well, dear," she said.

Amy and Ann had a very good holiday from the proceeds of the other items in the box that no-one had known about... and Ann had learnt that her friend had a very lucrative hobby indeed!

Barbara Robinson

Barbara has been a member of Carlisle Writers for more than ten years.

She was born in Threlkeld near Keswick, where she went to secondary school. She became a nurse in Carlisle. She is married, has three children and six grandchildren.

GBH

She was in despair. She never thought that this could happen to her. A respectable middle-aged woman, highly regarded in her own community sitting here in a prison cell. She felt ashamed but also slightly defiant. She thought, "If it happened again, I would do the same thing. Somewhere, somehow, somebody has to make a stand, even if it means brawling in the street!"

She had been dropped at the end of the road by her friends after a day out on the fells. It was already getting dark, and she had to pass a group of young men and girls who were further along the road. Suddenly, one of the group was knocked to the ground, and the rest set about him with feet and fists while he yelled for help. The girls were as bad as the boys. A sense of injustice flared and she remonstrated with one of the girls.

"Push off, you old bat!" was the response. "Mind your own business!"

By this time, the terrified youth lay on the pavement in a pool of blood. Suddenly, she was furious and she sailed in like a whirling dervish, her walking pole flying to left and right, and walking boots stamping on unsuspecting feet. Whack! Whack! Whack! Faces, arms, shoulders and backs. The attackers were momentarily bewildered by the sudden onslaught and, in amazement, stopped what they were doing.

"What do you think you're playing at, you old bitch!" shouted the most belligerent of the youths. By this time, neighbours were coming out of their houses, and someone had sent for the police who must have been near at hand as they arrived so suddenly.

"What's going on?" said the first policeman to get out of the car.

"It was her!" said one of the gang, a red weal appearing across his cheek. "She just started whacking us. Wait till my dad hears about this - you'll be for it!"

"They were all beating up this young man," she explained, pointing at the youth on the ground, who was now sitting up and nursing his injuries.

"Is this true?" asked the policeman.

"No, it was nothing," replied the victim, obviously too terrified to accuse anybody.

"Right, we will just take a statement from a few of you down at the station! The rest of you, get home now!"

All three of them - the woman, the injured youth and the chief protagonist - were ushered into the police car. At the police station, a slightly sympathetic sergeant said, "We'll have to put you in here for a while," as he put her into a cell.

She sat stunned for a while. She fingered a bloody lip. A stray fist must have split it. What was she going to tell her family? She'd have to gloss it over a bit, make light of it, or they'd never let her out of the house on her own again.

She became aware of one of the policemen looking at her through the spy window of the cell door. He came in and sat down opposite her. He took her name and address, asked her what she was doing on the street and why, and then told her that she was a very foolish woman. The victim had told them what had really happened. He was too frightened to press charges but was grateful that she had saved him from serious injury. But the other lad was threatening to sue her for assault.

'Please don't do anything like this ever again, Mrs Smith,' the policeman said. 'Did you know any of the youngsters involved?'

'No, I don't think so,' she replied, momentarily worrying about repercussions. 'What will happen now?'

'Well, if mi laddo *does* get his parents to sue you, you should get off with a caution. Unless you have any previous convictions. Have you?'

'No,' she answered, 'unless a speeding offence counts?'

'You'll be all right,' he said reassuringly. 'Mind you, if the Press get hold of it, they will have a field day! Now, come on, we'll drive you home.'

91

Grandma

I have the fondest memories of my Grandma. She was a small brown-eyed woman who always reminded me of a little bird.

She lived in a house with one cold tap, and that was about it. I cannot remember what the cooking arrangements were. The loo was down the yard in an outhouse; I think it was called an earth-closet. Every so often men used to go along the road, emptying them.

My Grandma brought up six children in this house, my aunts and uncles. There was another uncle, and I could never understand why he was called Uncle Billy Watson, and not Harrison like everybody else. Much later, I realised that he must have been born out of wedlock and brought up by grandma's sister.

Gran was one of those neighbourhood women who was always sent for in an emergency, such as a difficult birth or the laying out of a body. "Go for Jane Harrison!" would be the cry.

My father, my brother and I would walk across the valley to visit her on a Sunday morning. When I nodded off to sleep on the sofa, she would gently waken me up by sponging my face with a damp flannel before we faced the long walk back to the village. Granda Harrison was never much in evidence, and he died when I was seven.

As a treat, Grandma would give us a spoonful of condensed milk. I can see her yet in her floral pinny waving a spoonful at us! And as for Christmas visits, the table was always full of food, even though there was rationing in those days.

Life cannot have been easy for Grandma but I never saw her short-tempered or unwelcoming. She must have often been physically tired, but she always seemed to be bustling about, being hospitable. I don't remember her last illness - I must have been too busy with 'O' levels and all the other things important to a teenager, but I wish I had seen her to say goodbye. Grandma died when I was fifteen, the most loved of all my grandparents.

Reflections

Looking in the mirror at my own reflection,
Seeing all the marks of time, the hopes and the fears,
I try to raise myself from feelings of dejection
And think instead about the happy years.

The photographs of childhood holidays,
The picture postcards of exotic places,
"And look at this, I'd forgotten all about it,
A gang of us all pulling silly faces!"

And then a photo from a newspaper,
A little girl, and behind her head,
As plain as day a spaceman,
Who wasn't really there, the caption said.

Was he reflected from the moon or from the future?
Or from the past? A hologram, or maybe just a ghost?
Is all the world just a great reflection
Of other worlds? Or times to be? Or lost?

Trisha Nelson

Trisha is a long-standing member of the group. Her work in previous anthologies has appeared under the name Pan Allan. She now appears under her own name as she has recently produced a volume of stories and rhymes for children, *Trisha's Fishy Tales And Bugs On The Go*. Extracts from Trisha's book are included here. All profits from sales of *Fishy Tales* will be going to buy equipment for the children's unit at a local hospital.

Trisha was born in London. She is married and live in Eastriggs, near Gretna. In her time, she has been a PVC welder and a Brownie leader!

Larry the Naughty Lobster

"Larry, where are you?" his mother cried, "I have been looking everywhere for you." Naughty Larry came in just then.

"You have been told before," his mother said, "that you must not go off when it pleases you to. There is going to be a big fisherman's net coming soon as it is their fishing day. You will be caught and then I shall never see you again."

But naughty Larry was not taking any notice, so he didn't hear his Mummy's warning because he was thinking of something else at the time. "Bye, mum," he shouted to her, "I will see you later when I come back from my adventure."

Naughty Larry was messing about with something he had just found. It had big holes in it and he had gone and got his claws

95

caught. The harder he tried to get free the more he got tangled. Naughty Larry was getting frightened as he could feel himself being pulled further up to the top of the sea.

He wished with all his heart that he had heard what his Mummy was saying to him and then he knew that he would never see his Mummy again, because, you see, he never listened to his mother's warning.

Mrs Ladybird

Mrs Ladybird was flying around.
She stopped when she she saw something,
Sparkling on the ground.
She went to see what it could be,
And it turned out to be her own lost key.

The Greenfly

Greenflies have such big wings,
And they don't like to miss a thing.
Off to work they do go,
But it takes a long time because they're so slow.

Baby Moths

Two baby moths climbing up a wall,
Mummy shouts out "Please don't fall."
Up they struggle to the top,
When all of a sudden they begin to drop.

The Wasps

Wasps, wasps everywhere,
Flying in the garden, flying up the stairs,
Poking in the apples, clinging to the pears,
They do not know that the fruit is theirs.

The Funny Greenfly

Two funny greenflies sitting on a fence,
One was named Time and one was Dense.
Off they went for a fly in the sky,
Then Dense found out he could not fly.

Flies

Flies, flies everywhere,

They always seem to stop and stare,

Sitting on the tea pot,

Climbing up the spout,

Oh! I wish they would all clear out.

Marjorie Carr

Marjorie is a long serving member of the Carlisle Writers' Group and has served as its chairperson for many years. She enjoys the meetings as they can often inspire new poems, stories or even novels.

Marjorie is a published poet, but also writes short stories and novels. She has a love of arts and crafts, and is a nature lover, living as she does in a small hamlet north of Carlisle.

The Silver Locket

It was Sarah's twenty-first birthday and she wanted to buy something very special with the money her grandmother had given her. As she walked along the high street, for some inexplicable reason, she stopped at the antiques shop and began to look at the tray of jewellery in the window.

The shop had never drawn her attention before, probably, she thought, because she shared a little, one-bedroomed flat with her friend and workmate, Lisa. There was no room for grand pieces of antique furniture, or even the smallest of occasional tables, even if she could have afforded them, which she couldn't.

As she gazed at the tray, she noticed a silver locket lying half hidden under a gold gate bracelet. She had always wanted a locket although, being antique, it might be priced way beyond her grandmother's gift. There was a price tag but no matter how she strained and screwed up her eyes, she could not read it. She started to walk away, thinking it would cost too much, but then stopped. It wouldn't hurt to ask. She could always say it was too expensive. She turned back and entered the shop, the small bell above the door tinkling sweetly to announce her arrival. The shop was very cluttered with pieces of furniture, so she did not advance much further, for fear of knocking something over. She couldn't afford to pay for breakages, so she just stood in the small area next to the door.

As she waited for the owner to appear she could see the locket just around the corner but, although tempted, she didn't lean round to take it out and look at the tag; the owner of the shop might think she was trying to steal it in their absence.

"Can I help you?"

The voice of a softly spoken woman sounded almost as sweet as the bell and Sarah turned to see a slightly built old lady, wending her way towards her. She had to be all of eighty years, but her slim body passed along the narrow aisle between the furniture, as if she was a child of ten.

"I wondered how much the locket is?" said Sarah, pointing to the tray, but still rapt by the old lady's sprightliness.

"It's a lovely piece and very old," the lady commented, passing Sarah like a gentle breeze to lift the tray from the window. Setting it on a nearby table, she lifted the locket and placed it in Sarah's hand. Sarah was surprised by the weight of it.

"Pure silver," the lady said in her lyrical voice then, as she turned to leave, added, "It was made for you my dear. Have a good look."

"I just wanted to know the price," stammered Sarah, torn between looking at the tag and watching the old lady leave.

"I'm sure you will be able to afford it," the lady called back, as she disappeared between the stack of furniture.

Sarah felt awkward at being left alone again, especially as she had the locket in her hand. She quickly looked at the tag and couldn't believe her eyes. Her grandmother's money was just five pounds short of the asking price, so she didn't mind making up the difference. The chain alone was very strong and heavy, with each link carefully shaped. She gently brushed her thumb across the interlocking design on the front of the locket. Perhaps Celtic, she thought, or maybe a lover's knot. Prising open the locket, she looked at the fading sepia photographs - one, a pretty young woman and the other, a dashing young man. As she closed the locket and gazed at the design again, she heard someone approaching.

"Sorry to keep you waiting." The man suddenly gave her a sharp look with a voice to match when he added, "I see you managed to help yourself."

"I'll take the locket," she replied hesitantly, holding it out to him eagerly and taking out her purse from her bag.

He gave her a surly look but took it from her, saying gruffly, "I'll put it in a box for you." He then removed the price tag and placed the locket in a small box.

As Sarah handed over the money, she felt prompted to say, "Your mother was right. Please thank her for me."

"I'm afraid you are mistaken, madam. My mother is dead," he

replied, giving her a piercing glower.

"Sorry. I assumed . . . Never mind," said Sarah, somewhat flustered and unnerved by the gentleman and making a hasty exit, before making matters any worse.

Once on the street she wondered at the man. Why had he treated her like that? To have such a sweet old lady as his helper, she would have thought he could have been a little more pleasant himself. Still she thought, what had made her think it was his mother? Perhaps he did not like being reminded of his loss.

She was so excited she could not wait to show her grandmother what she had bought with the money. Sarah went straight round to her mother's house as, since the death of her grandfather, her grandmother had moved into her old room.

"Isn't it beautiful?" Sarah said, handing it to her grandmother.

"Very. My mother had one very similar."

"It has some old photographs inside." Sarah waited for her grandmother to don her spectacles, before opening the locket to show her, but the shocked look on her grandmother's face puzzled her. "What's wrong?"

"Well, I would never have believed it, but this is my mother's locket."

"Are you sure?" queried Sarah's mother.

"Oh yes. These pictures were taken shortly after my parents married. My father had the locket especially made," said the grandmother a little more calmly. "You'll find a picture just like it in the old album," she added pointing to the cupboard.

Sarah's mother brought out an old, leather-backed album. With the two women seated on the sofa, Sarah stood behind to peer over their shoulders at all the old photos.

"There," said her grandmother, indicating the picture in question.

"You're right," said the mother, adding, "They're exactly the same."

"Gosh. Fancy buying my great grandmother's locket and to think I nearly didn't go into the shop," said Sarah, amazed by the coincidence.

"Why was the locket never kept?" the mother asked.

"Probably one of my brothers got it. They were all wastrels and more than likely sold it to get some money," the grandmother said, still turning the pages.

Suddenly a photograph appeared which made Sarah's heart thump and she cried out, "Wait," with such force, that she startled the other two women.

"What?" said her mother, concerned by her daughter's sharpness of voice.

"Who is that lady there?" Sarah asked, her voice wavering with emotion.

"Your great grandma. It was taken just before she died," said her grandmother, wondering what was wrong with Sarah, as all the colour had drained from her face.

"It can't be. Are you sure?" queried Sarah, feeling faint and walking around the end of the sofa, to take a seat on the arm of it.

"What on earth is the matter, Sarah? You'd think you had seen a ghost," said her mother, staring with concern.

"I think I just have."

Sarah told them of the lady who had been in the shop. Her grandmother believed her, agreeing that Sarah's great grandmother had been soft spoken and nimble to the end. Sarah's mother, however, was more sceptical, saying lots of old ladies were like that and she could have been the gentleman's aunt, neighbour or friend.

"Then why didn't he correct me and say who she was; and why did he treat me so strangely? He must have thought I'd lifted the tray out of the window myself," said Sarah, beginning to see an explanation for his strange looks and comments.

"Go back and ask him," said her mother, still positive Sarah must be mistaken.

"No. Leave things as they are. You would feel a fool and be hard pressed to explain if there was no lady," said her grandmother wisely.

Sarah agreed. To her way of thinking, her great grandmother had wanted her to have the locket and, as it had now returned to the family, then that was all that really mattered.

The Game

Have you ever played the game where -

The more you win,

The less you gain?

The harder you try,

The less you succeed?

Solve one problem

Only to find another.

Fate's a fickle partner.

He deals the cards

With sleight of hand.

You play your best,

But he trumps it.

He can't be beaten,

So why play?

'Tis Art

'Tis art that makes the birds sing,
To brush colour into everything.
To spot and stripe, to splash and mould
The colours into nature's gold.

'Tis art that weaves the pretty nest.
To present each living thing at best.
To twine the grass, the flowers fair,
To thrive and live in nature's care.

'Tis art that drapes the stately trees
With leaves of every shape to please.
To paint the valleys, hills and skies
With greens and blues of nature's dyes.

'Tis art that makes the world go round,
To build and create upon the ground;
Houses, schools, factories, shops;
To harvest all of nature's crops.

John Nevinson

Since joining Carlisle Writers in 2010, John has written fiction for adults. Prior to this, he had a number of children's stories published – one was a runner-up in the *Independent* newspaper's Story Of The Year collection. His first anthology of short stories, *A Sting In The Tale,* is now available.

John trained to be a teacher in his home city of Liverpool before working in Carlisle primary schools for almost forty years.

As well as writing, John likes theatre, cinema, reading, walking, pub quizzes, gardening, local history and genealogy - he has traced his family tree back to 1723.

He Practised To Deceive

Oh, what a tangled web we weave,
When first we practise to deceive!
Marmion Sir Walter Scott

The trill of the telephone makes me jump. I'm very much on edge because of the secret wedding plans for Friday, and whenever the phone goes I am half expecting Fiona to call, saying that we have been rumbled.

We have managed to have a secret affair for the past two years while she has been skilfully steering through a divorce from her philandering husband, Bob. Fiona has cleverly maintained the image of the injured, suffering little wife - and Bob, chasing everything with a skirt and a pulse within ten miles of Carlisle, has been blissfully oblivious to it all. The deceiver will find he has been deceived! At times, it has been so hard to keep up *our* deception, and Fiona and I planned that sometimes we would not meet for weeks at a time to avoid any suspicion or detection. As soon as the decree goes through officially on Thursday, we can reveal everything with the next day's wedding - but before then we have to maintain the successful low profile. Fiona and I have plotted to keep it simple, so that no little hiccup can alter our plans.

But as the day approaches, I am as jumpy as a bird in a garden where cats prowl, so the shrill phone sounds incredibly loud.

"Yes. 817000." I am irritated at how tense I sound.

"Hello, Mr Baines. It's Lorraine."

"Lorraine?"

I cannot place the voice, and feel belligerently that this is another cold call about kitchens or insurance scams, so I am thrown when she says, "Lorraine from the garage. Hetherington's."

I vaguely remember the over-made up fortyish peroxide blonde behind the hatch who books in my BMW for its service. My car was checked over last week, in preparation for the honeymoon in North Wales, and all was fine.

"Is there a problem, Lauren?" I ask.

"It's Lorraine, Mr Baines. Er... Alan."

I am surprised at the use of my forename but I suppose she has all the business records in front of her.

"What's the problem?" I repeat.

"Well, er, Alan, there is no problem. Erm.....I hope you don't

108

think I am being too forward, but I wondered if you fancied coming out for a drink on Thursday evening?"

There is a stunned silence. Apart from this unexpected chat-up, I intend that any drinking on Thursday will be done with Fiona, to celebrate her ditching of Bob.

"Alan?" Her voice sounds a little more imperious. "I know you aren't seeing anyone, so I guess you are fancy free."

My God! Fiona and I have been so circumspect in our affair, everyone must think I am celibate and there for the taking. But nothing, *nothing* must interfere with all our two years of plans when they come to fruition on Thursday evening.

"Perhaps you would rather meet in a more intimate setting. I could make dinner." Lorraine is insistent now.

I flounder, and feel like a nine year-old explaining to a teacher why I don't have my PE kit.

"I am sorry, Miss er..."

"Lorraine!" she says forcefully.

"I'm afraid I have so much to do this Thursday..."

"Like what?" This woman is determined and ruthless.

"I... er..." Then the words tumble out. "I have an AA meeting at six o'clock."

"You're an alcoholic?" Lorraine gasps.

"Yes." I've shocked her. I *think* I am safe.

"Then there is no point going for a drink..." she reasons.

"No!"

"...So there's no problem, Alan. You will *definitely* come to my place for a meal, and we will have fruit juice."

She is intransigent.

"Er - and after that I meet my other counsellor," I burble.

"Your *other* counsellor!"

"Yes. He is helping me with my kleptomania. I steal from bookshops. I am banned from *Bookends* and *Waterstones*."

Oh, the lies are coming easily now, but already I am aware that I am going to get tangled up in the web somehow.

"You *steal!* And you see this man…when?"

"After AA. At eight o'clock."

"You see a counsellor at eight o'clock in the evening? Oh no! That is quite unbelievable. What kind of counsellor sees you at *that* time of night?"

"Erm… Because… Charlie and I are lovers!"

"What?" Her voice is now strained and cannot help but shriek.

"Yes. We have been an item ever since we were teenagers… and we set fire to the council gardening shed in Bitts Park. You have no idea how hard it's been to conceal this from everyone."

"Conceal it?" she gasps.

"It was a very expensive building," I whine ingenuously.

"You *dreadful* man!" Lorraine yells.

The phone slams down. Thank God! I am safe from that predatory witch.

*   *   *   *   *

Fiona phones on Wednesday evening.

"Alan? I was in *Whytes* coffee shop on St Mary's Gate today..." she begins.

"That new place? Nice spot."

"I heard a woman on the next table talking about the servicing of a plum-coloured BMW. As yours is the only one in Carlisle, I pricked up my ears, especially when she began to talk about the owner."

My heart begins to sink, and my mind goes blank.

"You assume she was talking about me," I suggest.

"The woman *was* talking about you, Alan. She told her friend that she has been carrying a torch for you for years. She has just discovered *amazing* things about you. The woman told her friend all about your secret life away from me - obviously those weeks when *you* suggested we play cool and act distant to avoid detection."

My mouth open and closes like a stranded fish gasping on a river bank. The words that spilled out so easily to Lorraine just won't form themselves for Fiona.

"It's over, Alan. I've dealt with one serial philanderer who was a crashing bore, but I just could *not* cope with a womanising, alcoholic, thieving, gay arsonist! Goodbye!"

"Why not add murderer to the list?" I thought, as I picked up the phone to make a date with Lorraine...

Bad Boys

I was the first one of the lads to pick up a stone and aim it at the heron. It fell just short of the bird, but the splash of water roused it from its concentration, and it flew off down the Eden with slow graceful beats of its large grey wings.

"Good try, Marcus!" shouted the lad who they always called Beefy.

The other boy stared at Beefy, wrinkling his nose and mouth as if he had eaten something disgusting. He was called Titch, and I never felt as easy with him as I did with Beefy.

"Good try?" mocked Titch. "That was a girl's throw, that was!"

I ignored the insult, knowing that Titch was only trying to provoke me into another argument, which he loved to do. Titch was so aggressive compared to Beefy. In the few weeks that I had known these lads, I realised that Titch made up for his small size with a sharp tongue and a fast temper. Beefy had been friendly almost at once, but I always felt that Titch was watching me, silently weighing me up, deciding to find out my weaknesses, and only too keen to play on them.

Titch knew that the insult about my weak throw would probably work. He was always making remarks about my accent, which was different from theirs, or my father's good job, saying it meant that I was bound to be soft and spoiled. It wasn't fair comment, but I knew that Titch was very close to discovering my secret. Yes, I was from a better, richer home than them. But I had needed to make new friends quickly in this strange new northern city, so I was determined to prove that I was a good member of the gang by being as rough and as naughty as they were. I knew that they were what my mother called 'bad boys' but somehow that made their company even more exciting, and made me more determined to be a proper member of the gang. I felt that Titch was close to discovering this.

Beefy scowled at Titch.

"At least he had a shot at the thing, mate. I didn't see you doing much!"

I didn't want them to fall out over me because that would destroy this small gang, and then I would be back just where I was five weeks ago, newly arrived in Carlisle with no friends.

"Look, lads," I said brightly, pulling a greasy package from a bag. "I've got something for us to eat."

I hoped this diversion for food would cool things down. Beefy happily took some of the sweetly-flavoured fruit cake and stuffed it into his greedy mouth. Titch squinted at me, his long brown hair flopping over his pale blue eyes.

"Did Mummy give you this, or did you bribe one of the servants?"

I sighed deeply. "I've told you before, Titch, we don't have servants."

He made a dramatic show of reluctantly eating some cake.

"I thought all you army families had people to wait on you, and work for you, and clean, and cook," he whined. "Most of all, *your* family. Wasn't your dad sent here specially? My brother has to work at the camp and reckons your old feller is the top man."

"My dad *is* high up at the camp, you're right. He was sent here specially from the south..." I began.

"But Marcus ain't in the flaming army, is he?" Beefy spluttered, crumbs shooting everywhere. "So lay off him, Titch!"

There was an awkward silence between the three of us. Then Beefy said one more thing to convince Titch that I was just like them.

"Look, Titch, just remember that Marcus got beaten by his father, just for knocking around with us..."

"Twice!" I interrupted.

"So I reckon if he gets that dished out by his dad, and yet still wants to be having fun with us, he's proved he is a good mate."

Silence returned. Titch finished the cake, sighed deeply and looked up the river towards Carlisle. The buildings were disappearing into a grey misty haze on this cool autumn day, and a pale watery sun was already dropping behind the trees. The only sound was that coming from the River Eden, high after heavy rain in the fells, and racing down towards the Solway. There was a steady rippling noise as it swirled through the branches of the trees already standing well out into the brown water. The treacherous river twisted and eddied, bubbling as if some giant hand was stirring it up below the surface.

"All right, all right!" Titch sounded convinced about me. "So what are we going to do next, lads?"

Since midday, we had been cheeky to an old woman and her son as they worked on their vegetable plot, and riled the furious man enough for him to come chasing after us. Seeing a lone fisherman, we had hidden in some scrubby bushes, throwing stones into the river to spoil his sport. We had covered up a deep puddle on a path with branches and leaves and watched to make sure that the next unwary walker got his feet wet. And we had tried to stone the heron. Next…

It was Titch's idea. And looking back, I should have guessed it was planned to put me in an awkward position. I should have known that Beefy's pleas for me to stay in the gang had irritated his old friend, who had munched treacherously through the cake which I had stolen from home, all the while plotting something nasty for me.

"Well, we have annoyed a few folks today, but we've done nowt exciting," said Titch quietly.

Stupidly, Beefy and I fell into his trap.

"What do you suggest?" I asked. What a fool!

Titch smiled. He pointed towards the branches of the trees, hanging over the swirling river. My stomach knotted. I just knew the skinny little weasel was going to suggest something dangerous and crazy, and I sensed that it was going to be a cunning test for me. No words needed to be said for me to realise that this plan had nothing to do with Beefy. It was between Titch and me.

I was standing up and walking towards the river bank before Titch had even explained what he planned. Beefy was a slow thinker but even he suddenly realised what was going to happen.

"No, Marcus! Don't be daft! My dad says this river is not to be trusted…" he blurted out.

It was just what Titch wanted to hear.

"Well, you might be a coward, Beefy, but I bet our brave army lad here isn't scared of climbing out along the branch as far as he can," he smirked.

I heard my voice saying, "Of course I'm not scared." I looked down at my feet as if they belonged to somebody else, amazed that they were walking steadily through the sticky brown mud towards the trees.

"Don't be stupid, Marcus!" begged Beefy. Things were moving too fast for his slow brain, but he knew in his heart that something bad was about to happen.

Titch watched me as I climbed into a tree which was on dry land. Then I reached awkwardly into the branches of one whose trunk was standing in the fast-flowing torrent. I transferred myself quickly from one tree to the other. Looking down, I could see water racing below me. I planned that I wasn't going to go too high up into the tree, as I knew the thinner branches would not support me. I found a sturdier branch lower down which, of course, put me nearer the crazily swirling waters of the swollen river. I lay as flat as I could and moved along the branch and out over the water. Already the wood beneath me dipped and sagged. I was vaguely aware that Beefy was yelling at Titch, pushing him and thumping him.

My heart was pounding and the sweat which plastered the hair to my head, poured down my neck. Dimly, I could see that Titch was standing with his arms folded, looking very pleased with himself, enjoying my danger, while Beefy was bellowing like an angry bull and running off through the soaking long grass.

I stopped moving and froze. I knew that I wasn't moving a muscle, yet I could feel that I wasn't staying still. There was the slightest, vaguest feeling that the branch was dipping towards the racing brown river, and that I was going along with it. Then above the sound of water crashing against the trunk, I could hear a creaking, tearing sound, and the branch bucked and tipped me forward. I fell into the river with an enormous splash. The last thing that I remembered was the coldness, the blindness, the roaring noise, the sensation of being crushed, going underneath the seething surface of the water, and the thump as I came up to the surface, hard against another tree trunk…

*   *   *   *   *

I stand in front of my father. In the past he has gone purple with anger and shouted, but this is more frightening. He is white with rage, and his voice is so quiet that I can hardly hear him.

"I will not waste time lecturing you, Marcus, as it does no good at all. I ask you not to mix with the locals but you do, knowing full well how it undermines my work here in Carlisle."

I open my mouth to explain, but he raises the palm of his hand to silence me, and withers me with an icy glare.

"Not a word, Marcus. You are lucky that one of my best soldiers was down by the river when that ridiculous fat boy came running for help. You were fortunate to be caught against a tree and not swept down the river to the open sea. My man was able to haul you to safety at a great risk to himself. But I have had enough, my boy! Quite enough!"

I flinch inwardly, thinking of another beating.

"How can I control these people when my own son disobeys me so openly? They will say, "He can control his soldiers at the garrison at Stanwix but not his eleven year-old son."

I stare at my father, wondering what comes now. His next sentence tells me.

"You will not remain in Britannia. When Maximus Servilius returns home to Rome next week, you will travel with him. I am enrolling you at a school there which is well-known for its strict discipline. Maybe *then*, you will start on the road to becoming a citizen of whom Rome can be proud. Now, out of my sight!"

I Don't Know How You Do It

It was Jake's stock answer to anything which Grace asked him to do.

"I don't know how to do it!"

Mending a fuse, retuning the television, fixing an outside light to a wall, replacing a section of damaged garden fence, checking a leaky washer... When Grace asked him to sort out the problem, Jake looked lost, and within thirty seconds was ploughing through the Yellow Pages for an electrician, a TV repair man, a carpenter or a plumber.

They were an unusual couple amongst their friends in that they got married without having lived together first, so whereas her sister Emily already knew that her husband Freddie was a control freak, Grace was shocked by Jake's incompetence and lack of desire to do things for himself. Or rather for themselves. Living in a creaking Victorian terraced house with groaning floors, draughty windows and a damp attic, there was a lot to do.

At first, Grace was tolerant of the army of plumbers and electricians who stayed for five minutes to do an easy job, but early one evening, as the lights once again flickered again and went out, she had had enough.

"Jake, those flaming lights again!" she shouted in exasperation.

"Well, it's a bit late for phoning *Livewires*," Jake moaned.

"What? Why phone *them*? Can't *you* sort it out?"

"Oh, babes, I don't know how to do it!" he whined.

"If you want to watch that bloody football match at eight o'clock…" Grace began.

"Oh, if they're still off by then, I'll go to the Red Lion," he said.

It was the straw and the camel's back time for Grace.

"Okay, darling. You just go and sit happily in the pub and see the match and I will do some knitting in the dark," she hissed.

"If you don't mind?" he half-questioned her.

The fact that her sarcasm had been lost on Jake was the match to Grace's blue touch paper.

"Mind? *Mind?* Of course I bloody mind!" she shrieked.

Jake looked genuinely surprised at the outburst.

"It's not my fault the lights went out…" he began.

"I know that…"

"But I don't know how to do it," he finished.

The cardboard box hit him just below the eye, and the only sound that could be heard in the shocked semi-darkness was chocolates skittering across the pine floor.

"You are *so* right. You don't know how to do anything," she spat.

Jake, rubbing his cheekbone, was suddenly animated.

"Men don't have the monopoly on mending fuses and fixing washers! We aren't born knowing the colour codes for changing a plug! What's wrong with *you* sorting them, instead of always expecting me to do it? I thought you were supposed to be a liberated twenty-first century professional woman!"

Grace hadn't ever heard Jake put so many coherent sentences together at one time, and her retort was quick.

"And you are a nineteenth century throwback!"

*   *   *   *   *

Jake moved back to his parents three days later. Grace went to a house maintenance course at the local night school, found a taste for it, and within two years left the bank, and set up her own business. *Grace's Favour* tackled washers, plugs, blocked sinks, problem fuse boxes… And its publicity made it very clear that it responded only to calls from women, no helpless men.

Grace was gratified when her female clientèle said in awe, "I don't know how you do it!" and she would reply, "Actually, it was my ex-husband who encouraged me!"

Anne Carter

Joining the group this year, Anne has worked in the theatre in the UK and California. She was born in Cockermouth and educated here, in France and the United States. She has married twice; her first husband was an American, and they have one son who lives in Los Angeles. She has two grandchildren.

Anne studied Russian ballet in Britain and France, and studied drama in Britain and New York. She studied sculpting, languages and sports science; she also worked in law in this country. Locally, she directed the Mary Queen of Scots section of the 1977 pageant at Carlisle Castle.

Cross Purposes

"Mr Smith, I presume?"

"Actually, no. Mr Riabonshinka."

The smaller man did not understand and wanted to know the name of the man standing before him, but the man standing before him had no intention of revealing his real identity because, clearly, he was not Mr Riabonshinka.

Or so thought the very English Mr Russell Blair, old Etonian, Oxford educated and owner of Newtonly Manor. He was also second-in-command of MI7, and had been appointed by another Etonian, Oxford educated and owner of Chateau Monteil, from whence he used to arrive by helicopter to attend meetings at headquarters. Quite often he used to stay for the weekend with Mr

Russell Blair at his castle.

Mr Russell Blair decided to try again.

"Are you an associate of Mr Smith?"

"Je ne connais pas Mr Smith," the man replied.

This really threw Mr Russell Blair. One had vaguely paid tribute to French lessons at Eton, but one had never learned the stupid language. One had learned to recognise it, but that was all. Everyone spoke English as far as Mr Russell Blair was concerned, and if one didn't, then one should jolly well learn it! In fact, he was pretty sure it should be made compulsory.

"We do not speak other languages at MI7, and that is why I shall refer to you as Mr Smith."

"But I am not Mr Smith. I am Mr Riabonshinka. I speak several languages."

Mr Russell Blair was beginning to get very irritated by this stupid man's insistence that he was not Mr Smith.

"What does your wife call herself?" he asked.

"Svetlana," replied the man.

This was getting far too complicated for Mr Russell Blair who almost shouted that he wanted to know her surname.

"Mrs Riabonshinka, of course. In my country it is normal for the lady to take her husband's surname when they are married."

Mr Russell Blair did not know what to do. He could hardly accuse the man of lying, so he decided to consult with his old friend at Chateau Monteil. He excused himself, went into the next room and asked head office to put him through to the Chateau. A secretary replied, only to tell Mr Russell Blair that his master was attending a dinner at the Ukrainian Embassy in London. It occurred to Mr Russell Blair that if his friend had been invited, he should have been invited too. It was just not cricket!

He decided to go back and make another attempt, but before he could get started the man got up and demanded to speak to the Prime Minister. Mr Russell Blair was apoplectic.

"We do not do things that way in our country!"

"It would be better if you allowed me to use your telephone, so that I can make sense of this situation more expediently," said the man.

Mr Russell Blair was now so exasperated that he lost his temper. "Get out! Get out!" he shouted, whereupon the man left.

A couple of hours later, Mr Russell Blair's phone rang, and a very agitated Prime Minister told him that Mr Riabonshinka had felt so insulted that he had now cancelled Mr Russell Blair's invitation to the Ukrainian Embassy's dinner. He added that the Queen was very displeased because Mr Riabonshinka was a distant cousin of hers!

A Very Dangerous Double

Karanin replaced the receiver and gazed at the telephone for a moment. Robert had said that she need not pick him up. He would get a lift home. She remembered that she had to go to town to get some marmalade. She was on the point of ringing him back when she decided just to turn up. She left the bedroom and ran down the cantilever staircase, through the open front door and down the entrance steps to her car.

She arrived ten minutes later at the car park and noticed, unusually, the office door was closed. She took out her key, opened the door and closed it behind her. It was dark in the hall but she knew her way to Robert's room. She could hear a noise she could not identify on the other side. It was not voices. She would surprise him. She quietly opened the door, her eyes resting on the big mirror. She was frozen to the spot. Robert and a young man were kissing each other passionately, so passionately that they could not possibly notice anything else. The reflection would always be stamped on her memory.

Karanin seemed to have been standing there for an eternity and then quietly she closed the door. Shock turned to numbness, then fury, and then she felt tears rolling down her cheeks. On looking back, she did not remember getting to her car. She started the engine, drove straight out of the car park. She must pull herself together. She must concentrate. She must get back home to think. She turned onto the road that would take her back to the village but she was shaking so much she pulled into the first lay-by outside the town.

Who was the young man? How long had Robert known him?

Suddenly she remembered. It had been the evening of the honeymoon and they had gone down to the hotel bar which overlooked the sea, to have a drink before dinner. She sat by the window and Robert went to get the drinks. She was watching the sun set, but something made her turn round towards the bar. Robert was gazing into the eyes of a young man who was returning the gaze. At the time, she had dismissed the incident but in her heart of hearts she knew it wasn't just her imagination. She had never had any cause to reflect on it until now.

Had there been others? How could she face him again? What would she say?

Oh my God! What was going to happen to Patrick? He was only seven and he was a very happy child.

Karanin had been married before. She and Frank had both been very young and had enjoyed travelling. There was nothing gay or bisexual about Frank and nothing ever seemed to be wrong until they thought they should settle down together; after marriage little or nothing seemed to be right. Responsibility did not lie easy with immaturity. She often thought of Frank with affection. She thought about him now. If only...

Cars passed by in a steady stream. Everyone was returning from work and she knew she must get back home because Patrick would be home from school. She got into the line of traffic and was home in five minutes only to be met by Angela, the au pair, who was in a terrible state. All her words were tumbling out at once and eventually Karanin realised what she was saying. Angela had saddled up the pony for Patrick on his return from school, which was the usual procedure, when suddenly a low-flying plane came over and the pony took fright, galloping off down the back drive with Patrick on her back. Angela had been powerless to do anything. It had only been a few minutes ago. She had tried to phone Robert but there had been no reply. Karanin did not stop to think. She was still in the car and set off down the back drive, trying to imagine which way the pony would go. By this time she could think of nothing else but Patrick. She did not know which way to turn, but decided to try one road at a time. It seemed that she had been driving for hours when suddenly she came across the pony munching grass; Patrick was sitting on the verge crying. She drew up at the side of the road and ran to Patrick, hugging him.

"Darling, are you all right?"

"Yes, mummy. I fell off. It wasn't Daisy's fault. It was that noisy plane. She must have been very frightened."

Karanin just kept hugging him. She realised she must get her son back home and she must find somewhere safe for Daisy until she could be collected later. There was a house a few yards away. She went to the door and knocked. A young woman answered. Karanin told her what had happened and the sympathetic woman agreed to take care of Daisy until she could be picked up. Karen thanked her and she and Patrick drove home. Karanin intended to leave the boy with Angela and return to pick up Daisy in the horse-box.

When they arrived home, Angela was so relieved to see them. She took Patrick in to have his tea and Karanin set off again. Once she got Daisy home, she would take Patrick to the doctor to make sure all was well.

With the pony back in her stable and Patrick given the all clear by the doctor, Karanin's thoughts strayed back to Robert. She knew she couldn't live with this situation. What would happen to their lives?

"Mummy, is Daisy all right?"

"Darling, Daisy didn't fall. You're the who one who fell. She's fine."

"I know, but she ran so fast she must've been terribly frightened."

"Yes, but she was nibbling grass when I arrived so she must've calmed down."

Angela brought in the tea things and said, 'Mr Blakestone rang and said he would be little late. He thought you might like to go out to dinner. He's booked *The Sandpiper* for 8pm. I told him what had happened and that Patrick seemed to be all right. He thought you would welcome a night out after Patrick went to sleep. He said there's no need to call him if these arrangements are okay. He should be here by 7.15.

Karanin could not have picked up the phone to call him back. She wondered what she was going to say to him when he arrived.

"That will be all right, Angela," she murmured. "Let's get Patrick's his supper. Are you hungry, darling?"

"I am a bit, now." Patrick said. "Can I have ice-cream tonight?"

"Yes, darling. For pudding." Karanin thought the must be all right

129

if he could manage ice-cream.

After she'd put Patrick to bed, she went to her room to change. Why on earth was she doing this? She looked at the clock. He'd be home in quarter of an hour. She didn't want to dress up. She needed to talk to him here. She needed a drink but if she had one, her head wouldn't be clear and it did need to be clear.

She put on a black dress. She was in mourning. She restored her make-up and slowly went down the staircase. She caught sight of herself in the mirror. She looked pale. As she reached the hallway, the front door opened and Robert stood there with the young man. She thought she would faint.

"Karanin, darling. I've brought one of my favourite clients to dine with us at *The Sandpiper*. This is Carl. He's been longing to meet you ever since I told him that you were more attractive than the photograph on my desk."

It seemed as if time had stopped still. The young man was gazing at her intently and intimately. He held out his hand and said, 'You're right, Robert. Far more than I could ever have imagined.'

Karanin automatically held out her hand, which he took and held up to his lips while still gazing at her. She realised she was staring back at him.

"Come in, Carl. We'll have a drink. Angela can drive us and can pick us up afterwards." He moved into the drawing room and Carl stood back to let Karanin follow.

This was a nightmare; it can't be happening, was all she could think.

"What about Patrick?" she asked.

"Oh, we can get Mrs D. to come in for a few minutes," Robert replied.

"No, we can get a taxi," Karanin said. "He's had a shaking up today."

What was Robert doing, bringing him into the house? Why does Carl look at me as if he fancies me? He's very handsome. Oh God, it's all so unbelievable. Why am I going out to dinner with the two of them? She tried to be polite, which seemed to attract Carl more than ever. Robert didn't seem to notice. He was his usual charming self. She heard little of the conversation and spoke less, not being able to think of anything to say. She sat in the taxi with the two men. She heard Carl say, while still gazing at her, "You're very lucky, Robert."

She ate little and drank only water. They returned and Robert suggested Carl stay the night. She went to bed.

During the next few months the divorce was arranged. The house was sold and ancillary matters concerning Patrick were settled. Karanin didn't want Patrick spending time with his father. Robert did not contest the divorce and she was well provided for. She decided to go back to work when Patrick went away to school.

It was six years later when Karanin met Ewan, an estate agent who was quite a lot younger than her. Robert had been older. They started living together and Patrick seemed to like him. They went together to Mauritius for a holiday and Ewan asked her to marry him. She felt she was not yet ready to marry again, though sexually they were very suited. They fitted together well as a family. Patrick thought he was a good buddy. Patrick mattered; as he got older he might resent another man.

After a quiet wedding, Karanin and Ewan went to Cornwall for a short honeymoon. Their hotel was lovely; overlooking the sea. Once they'd settled in, they made love and then went for swim.

"What would you like for dinner tonight, Karanin?" Ewan asked her. "Shall we have some champagne?"

"Lobster," she replied, "with a lovely big salad. And 'yes' to the champagne too."

They dressed for dinner, she in a delightful white dress. "So full of hope," she said. He looked terribly handsome in his white shirt and blue slacks.

They arrived at the bar and Ewan went to get their champagne, while she browsed the menu. She looked up to see if he was coming back and suddenly froze. Ewan was gazing into the eyes of a young man standing at the bar. The man turned round and looked straight at her.

It was Carl.

Happy Birthday

The girl sat there, staring. A chorus of *Happy Birthday* rang out from the assembled crowd. A cake with candles was placed in front of her. She just stared.

"Come on! Blow them out!" the crowd roared.

She just sat there, staring. She could hear what they were saying, but she could not react. She thought how like a crowd of clowns they were and wondered if they were there to entertain her. Where was the ringmaster?

She gazed through the candlelight and the thought occurred to her that it must be like gazing into a crystal ball. The more she gazed, the less she heard, and gradually a scene presented itself before her.

She could see a lake and mountains, and a lovely sailing boat on the lake. She began to feel the heat of the sun and noticed that the blueness of the sky was reflected in the lake as if it were a mirror. Passing clouds animated the picture.

She was distracted by another movement. A man was waving to her, but she could not make out who he was.

"Come closer. I want to know who you are."

The boat came over to her and he held his hand out to her to welcome her aboard. She knew it was *him* even though he did not utter a word. He began to play the violin and they sat gazing at each other. She knew the music. It was Paganini. The music was leading her into another picture. She sat watching him play. She was thinking, "This must be heaven. How is it possible to create such a sound?"

She got up and began to dance. Her ballet shoes carried her away, interpreting the music. They were both in an enormous opera house. He was playing and she was dancing. The faster he played, the faster she danced. She felt the sheer ecstasy of the blessedness at the heart of things. There was nothing like it in heaven or on earth. She knew she had met paradise.

"I don't want the music to stop!" she cried out.

Buts as with all things, nothing lasts for ever. She felt she was twirling in an ever-increasing spiral as the violin music rose to a crescendo. She could see the music and the dance disappear into the distance. He waved to her. She waved to him. She heard someone say, "He just died." He shouted, "Wait for me!"

She felt as if she was caught up in a tangle of bushes, and was struggling to get through. She heard a voice say, "Just a few more birthdays left, and you will be here with me."

She blew out the candles, and thanked everyone.

That night, as she fell asleep, she returned to her dream. But she knew it was not really a dream. It was life itself, and she knew she did not have to wait too long to be with him again. In knowing this, she slept peacefully until the wait was over.

Roberta Twentyman

Roberta was born and brought up in the Borders. Now retired, she lives in Cumbria. Her work is often inspired and influenced by the places where she has lived and worked, both at home and abroad as well as the people she has met.

Several of her short stories have been published. Novels *Daisychain* and *In Another Life* are to be followed by a children's story book later this year.

A Voice From The Past

Dear Penny,

I know it's not my turn to write but believe me, you'll want to hear about this little incident, toot sweet! I know, I know – I should have kept up the French.

Anyway, you know how every now and again life throws you a googly, and your equilibrium is shot to hell for a few days? That's what happened to me the other day, a real bolt from the blue.

As you know, shopping has never been high on my list of enjoyable experiences – any kind of shopping. I've always been one of those know-what-I-want, buy-it and-get-home-asap sort of shoppers, much to your constant dismay. In the supermarket I *do* try and create a menu as I go along. What food for which day of the week and… (you can stop sniggering Penelope… it keeps me from slitting my wrists) and my mind does tend to wander. Inevitably, I tend not to see people unless they give me a prod.

So I got quite a fright, when all of a sudden I was jolted from my dream-like state and back to reality by a voice from the past. A voice that jarred every nerve-ending in my body, a voice with the same buttock-clenching effect of chalk screeching on a blackboard.

My attention focused and then honed in on a face deep in concentration over the purple broccoli. 'The voice' was arguing the merits of organic versus cost with anyone who happened to be passing by.

I knew that voice and I knew that face. It took a few minutes of racking my brain to remember where from. She wasn't a relative, or a friend, or an acquaintance that I hadn't seen for a while. I couldn't place her at work either. I trolled through a mental list of people I knew from various committees and groups – no, no one came to mind.

The purple broccoli was discarded and she headed for the cheese counter. I had to follow. It drives me crazy when menopausal mania keeps me from remembering even the most trivial of things… doesn't it you? Anyway, I had to get to the bottom of it.

At first I thought perhaps she was the mother of one of our Jessica's friends… again no one sprung to mind. By the way, you'll be pleased to hear she's got over her Goth fetish – at least now she doesn't look gangrenous!

Had I worked with her in the past? I thought I'd cracked it – she was that awful wife of my boss when I worked at Harpers. You know, the one who always called her husband 'Mister'… but – no, she was much too tall.

Suddenly, she doubled back and was heading straight towards me. Not wanting to be caught staring, I lowered my eyes as she passed by. That's when it clicked. It was her ankles, one thicker than the other with a slight scar. I *knew* those ankles. Those ankles haunted me from school days. Now I knew why that scary voice had struck such a persistent chord.

Memories came flooding back. Isn't it strange how something trivial can act as a trigger? *You'll* remember her. She was my worst enemy at school – only after she'd made a play for Reg, and I naturally sought revenge. Do you remember Reg, my first love? He married Babs Dockray eventually, you know, the one with the Elastoplast over one lens! Okay – okay, I'll get on with it, I can hear you huffing from here! But not yet! I'll give you another clue.

Picture this: Saturday morning on the school hockey field, middle of November, freezing our tushes off in a practice match. You were goalie that day 'cause Rene Baxter was off with period pains – again – and you were livid. Anyway, I was swinging full welt at a cross ball when my stick 'somehow' connected with her ankle. There was an enormous crack, a piercing scream and she dropped like a stone.

I didn't stop to commiserate; we were one down with only a few minutes to go. You know what it was like... that sort of thing happened practically every match, we all had battle scars. Another clue – she was well known as a bit of a wuss when it came to a tackle.

Next thing we knew, play had been stopped. The P.E. teacher (remember Dipsy Mottram?) was called on, and the rest of the girls gathered round to assess the damage. All except us that is. You and I took the opportunity to have a quick fag behind the goals.

Turned out I'd broken her ankle. Well actually, it was only a hairline fracture. God, the fuss she made was incredible. Even old Mottram told her to put a sock in it. Dipsy's dead now by the way, just before Christmas… had a stroke and fell off her bike – or visa versa.

Where was I? Oh yes! Remember you laughed like a drain when her mother complained to mine about my less than sportsman-like conduct, which I vehemently denied of course? As if! Well, from that day on there was no love lost between us I can tell you.

And there she was, in Tesco's, by now examining deodorant. I'm glad she found a use for that at last! I hadn't clapped eyes on her for – what? Must be thirty years.

As I roamed the aisles after her, I couldn't help but wonder, as you do, you know… How had her life mapped out? What sort of a career did she have? Had she married and if so – who? Was it someone we'd known at school? Did she have kids? How was her ankle?

I toyed with the idea of tapping her on the shoulder and, you know, saying, 'Hi, Marion, remember me? Liz Martin that was?'

Yeah, that's right. You've got her. Of course it was… it was Marion Bissett. 'Russet Bissett'. All red hair and halitosis. And a voice box carved out of granite.

Well, in the end I decided perhaps not – tapping her on the shoulder that is – probably best to leave well alone. She always was the needy type and I couldn't be bothered. My equilibrium is almost back to normal. Yeah… I reckon now and again it's wise to bite your tongue, and just keep on wondering. Don't you?

Sorry I've had to resort to typing letters. It seems arthritis is definitely here to stay; writing anything more than a couple of sentences is nigh on impossible. I do miss pen and ink though.

How's Ted's knee by the way? Had his cartilage op yet? I thought living in Hong Kong he'd be into Tai Chi. Not still trying to re-live his glory days in the Sunday league, is he? They never grow up do they?

Until the next time.

Love 'n' stuff.

Liz

The West Wind

David's footsteps were muffled by the fresh fall of snow as he left the Indian lodge. His eyes automatically scanned the horizon. He stood still for a moment or two and gazed in wonder. Beyond the rustic cabins and reindeer-skin tepees, the snow-clad mountains soared up into the vast blue-black sky, where a never-ending network of brilliant stars twinkled back at him. Alaska, or, as the Indians called it, the Land of the Long Night.

As an incomer, he knew it would be a long time before he would be accepted, but his skills as a doctor had made him most welcome. However, David felt those skills to be somewhat lacking at the moment, though he couldn't put his finger on why.

He mulled over what his last patient, Tak, had said as he finished examining him. "Don't worry, Doc. It'll soon be over."

David's mind had wandered, thinking back to his text books, searching for an answer. He noticed Tak grinning at him.

"Sorry? What?" he asked.

Tak smiled, his wrinkled old face a roadmap of his life.

"I believe you white folk call it malaise. You know, being all edgy and irritable. But don't worry, it's only old Tornuaq."

David was intrigued. As well as ordinary everyday ailments, each patient this last week appeared to be headachy, anxious, agitated. So was he, but *his* he put down to being permanently cold, hungry and tired. And just to confirm it his stomach rumbled noisily. He raised an eyebrow. "Old Tornuaq?"

"Yessir. A spirit that messes with your head as the pressure builds under the ice."

David pursed his lips and waited, not sure whether Tak was taking the mick or not.

Tak continued. "Soon the Great Spirit Atka will come and loosen the side of the grey cloud tent above, to let in Unalaq, the West Wind from another world. Then at the first sound of the ice cracking, Tornuaq will leave." He stared out of the bare window and across the vast frozen lake. "About nine or ten days, I reckon."

The doubt on David's face must have been obvious, though he had found some of these old Indian myths and legends had a habit of holding more than a grain of truth.

"You'll see," insisted Tak. "Has done since the beginning of time, since the Great Spirit carried away the sun and the moon, leaving only ice and cold and snow."

As he took his leave, the stillness almost crackled with tension as David revved the engine and turned up the heat in the Land Rover.

At the far end of Main Street, right on the edge of town where civilisation tailed off and wilderness took over, The Moose Tooth Pub welcomed all-comers. The only place in town where you could have a few beers, a game of pool, watch the latest ice hockey game, eat a hearty meal, and surf the net. The incongruity made David chuckle.

Outside the pub, he could just make out Tammy Wynette lamenting her *D.I.V.O.R.C.E.* on the jukebox. The mouth-watering aroma of things cooking assailed his taste buds. He knew the menu off by heart: caribou stew, simmered for hours in red wine and infused with dried herbs; moose and reindeer steaks, two inches thick, cooked to order and smothered with whatever sauce chef had on the back burner. A strong palette was needed to cope with the chilli, and the burgers – well, they just melted in the mouth. All accompanied by sour-dough bread, and *all* of mammoth proportions.

He longed for summer, and healthier options. Cold water seafood, such as copper river salmon with its rich nutty flavour, and king crab, so big that just one could feed a whole family. Chef had been quick to reassure him there would also be enough elk and bear to satisfy a proper appetite!

As he entered the building, Tammy Wynette's pain came to an end. The draught from the open door caused a few leaves from the dried herbs hanging off the rafters to drift slowly down. However, the normal clatter and chatter were absent. Here, again, a tense, eerie quiet prevailed. The coffee machine hissed steam from the far end of the bar as several heads turned his way, nodded, and went back to their own business.

The chef leaned against the jamb of the open kitchen door, massaging his temples. Rick, the owner, looked up from his newspaper, stubbed out his cigarette and dragged himself back behind the bar

"The usual, Doc?"

David nodded, while counting his loose change out over the counter.

Rick noted the tired, drawn face, the anxious eyes and the

agitation.

"Won't be long now," he smiled reassuringly.

"So I've heard," said David grinning. "At the first sound of the ice cracking."

He shook his head, hardly able to believe he had actually uttered those words.

Rick slid the foaming glass of beer across the bar.

"No kidding, doc. *I* didn't believe it either, when I first came. When it goes, it booms and echoes down through the passes, across the creeks and crackles on right through town. Pressure'll be gone. Spirits lift within minutes. You'll see."

David raised an eyebrow, but resisted making any comment.

A glance round the room settled on the unmistakable figure of Toben Millit, a local trapper; all 6 foot 7 and 23 stone of him, perching precariously on a three legged stool. He concentrated anxiously on the screen in front of him. Several others hovered nearby, peering over his shoulder. David joined them, curious to see what they were looking at.

The screen kept renewing itself with multiple weather maps, criss-crossed by an explosion of lines and numbers. *National Weather Service, Alaska* flashed boldly on and off. The maps suddenly disappeared and a bronzed, dazzlingly white-toothed presenter's face, loomed in their place, the smile never wavering once not even when reading from the auto-cue.

"Broad, low pressure over the northern Alaskan coast will move toward Banks Island this week. Further south, high pressure will spread rapidly across the coast behind the low, bringing strong westerly winds. Yup, summer's around the corner, folks! Temperature, including the wind chill factor, is a balmy 28 below! If I were a betting man, I'd put money on it being maybe only three weeks till the first ice cracks."

Toben frowned, "Horse manure! Where's Tak? What does Tak say? You seen him, Doc?"

"Today," sighed David. "He said nine or ten days."

Toben nodded. "Nine or ten days it is then."

Nine days, ten hours and thirty-five minutes later, the Great Spirit Atka allowed Unalaq, the West Wind, in under the cloud. The sound of the ice cracking boomed and echoed down through the town, and Tornuaq departed.

Twisted

I clapped and sang as enthusiastically as everyone else, while watching the guests circle the bride and groom. They sat on ordinary wooden chairs, each holding one end of a scarf. The Hora had begun.

Alan explained that Orthodox Jews were not allowed to touch each other while they dance; with this special dance they could connect, without physical contact. A bit rich I thought, having watched them snog the face off each other a couple of nights before.

Suddenly, the couple were hoisted into the air. 'Mazal Tov', we all cheered. I glanced at Esther. Her cheeks were flushed, her eyes dancing – but they were not following the bridal pair, they were fixed on Alan.

A cold hand clutched my heart. This was all going to end in tears.

It had all started a couple of months before, when Alan had asked me to go to his cousin's wedding with him. I jumped at the chance. I'd never been to a Jewish wedding. It would be fun. Though being mid-week, it meant using up precious holidays. 'Whose daft idea was it to get married on a Wednesday?' I queried. 'Why not Saturday like everyone else?'

Alan sighed, "Oy vey... that's Shabbas, dumb-dumb."

He tolerated my ignorance of Judaism surprisingly well. However, there was a catch. I should have known there would be. Al wanted me to pretend to be his girlfriend. He was sick to death of his family haranguing him about his love life, or lack of one, whenever he went home.

"It's only for three days," he pleaded. "All expenses paid."

Three days? An evening I could cope with – but three days! After much begging and bribery I relented. It was the bribery that clinched it. Dinner at whichever restaurant I wanted, but really that only meant any pizza place back in D.C. – and I'm not that fond of pizza - or theatre tickets, which meant the local Am Dram, where Alan was the star turn. And to be honest he wasn't *that* good; he could sing, but he couldn't act for toffee. Another bribe was that he would do my ironing for a whole month and, at a push, clean my oven. *Now* he was talking! Two of the domestic jobs from hell! These clinched it. Of course, I gave in.

On the flight he filled me in with details of his relatives. His Uncle Michael was to be avoided at all costs; he was known to hit on anything with a pulse. But Uncle Saul was a sweetheart. Aunt Miriam was strictly Orthodox and should be given a wide berth or she'd interrogate me to death. He reckoned she was secretly Mossad!

Were they kosher? Yes. No ham sandwiches, then. Bagels, latkes and chicken soup here we come!

Then, of course, there was his grandmother. Alan absolutely adored Esther and she was the one who gave him the most grief about. "Find you a nice girl – make ze family!" It was the only thing that would make her happiness complete.

He quickly donned his yamulke as we walked the concourse in New York. He was on home ground now and conforming. More to the point his father, Benjamin, was picking us up.

I, on the other hand, was getting more anxious by the minute.

Al grinned. "Don't worry. They'll just be pleased I've found a nice Jewish girl."

I stopped dead in my tracks. "I am *not* pretending to be Jewish, Alan," I screeched. "That's bloody stupid." In fact, it finally dawned on me that the whole idea was a bloody stupid one.

Alan ignored my panic. "You might need to kiss me a couple of times in public – just to make it look good," he added quickly, as he waved to his father beyond the barrier. That would be no problem; I often hugged and kissed him. Sensing my train of thought he added, "And I don't mean as a friend. I mean real smackeroos!"

I shuddered. That was going a bit far. But then again... a month's ironing and a clean oven for just a couple of kisses? Okay, I could cope with that. "Oh, all right. But no tongues or I'll rearrange your genitals." How shallow can you get! What was I saying? What was I thinking about? That's just it though, isn't it – at nineteen you don't think too much; at least at that moment I didn't seem able to – and I was sober!

Benjamin moaned about the wedding all the way home to the Lower East Side. He detested weddings. He hated his sister-in-law and couldn't stand her husband but he loved his niece. He was going to get shickered.

I consoled myself with the knowledge that at least I didn't have a mother to contend with. In my experience *they* were usually the fly in the ointment. His mother, Ruth, had passed away some years

147

before, so there was just his Dad and Grandmother; Bobeshi, as Al called her

As an afterthought he warned, "She takes a bit of getting used to. About every fifth word is Yiddish!"

"Great," I muttered between gritted teeth. I was used to Alan's occasional weird way with words, but not every fifth word!

"But don't worry," he attempted to reassure me, "you'll soon catch on." I actually saw him cross his fingers! "You're a lot like her in spirit!" he added quickly.

Hell's bloody bells! Somehow that didn't help.

"Shalom," Grandmother Esther said as we shook hands.

Once pleasantries had been addressed and the trip up from D.C. discussed, we finally sat down.

Suddenly she asked, "Why you speak so funny? You have ze problem wid ze English too, heh?"

My hackles rose, my spine stiffened. The idiot hadn't bothered telling them? Well, I'd had enough of Limey jokes and nobody's Granny frightened me, whatever the language! "Actually, Mrs Goldstein. I *am* English, but fortunate enough to have a Scottish mother. I can retreat into the vernacular if you prefer," I replied.

Alan quickly leapt in. "Stop teasing her, Bobeshi. You know I already told you Sally is from the UK."

She chuckled. "Oy vey, the poor soul! Never mind, is not your fault," she said to me. "I shall call you Sarah – a good Hebrew name."

My very British hackles were still standing on end, but as my real name was Sarah I conceded and gave a thin smile. "That's fine with me, Mrs Goldstein. And I shall call you Hester."

Alan coughed, as she spluttered and cackled, "Oy vey," and laid a hand on my arm. "Motek, my name is *Esther*, but you can call me Bubbe, if you like."

I raised an eyebrow, "Indeed. Esther it is then."

She turned to Alan, her face suffused with love for her only grandchild. "Aaron my darlink, at last, you've found a…" she too raised an eyebrow, "nice Jewish girl. Yes?" and looked me up and down. She sucked in air behind her teeth and shook her head, "But no hips. Not good for ze bubelas."

I hovered between being flattered and insulted. No hips! I settled on flattered, as there was absolutely no way I would be having Alan's babies anyway!

Alan? Aaron! His name was Aaron? He'd never told me that. But before *Aaron* could lie his socks off, I quickly pointed out, "And I'm not Jewish either, Esther."

Suddenly her whole attitude changed. She actually beamed at me, and shouted down the hallway, "Benjamin! She's a goy! And she's English! What will your sister-in-law Miriam say about that, heh?" She chuckled mischievously, her eyes sparkling at whatever devious thoughts were flitting through her mind.

Benjamin joined us; he had obviously been listening and was smiling broadly. "And she has chutzpah. I might enjoy this wedding after all," he laughed, gathering me into a bear-like hug.

After the inevitable, but delicious chicken soup, Esther took me by the hand and led me into the living room. "Tell me, Sarah. Are you twisted?" she asked.

I was stunned. I mean she hardly knew me. I marvelled at her insight. I loved this woman; she was a gem. We were on the same wavelength. I was speechless.

"Nu? Are you twisted?" she asked again impatiently.

I looked to Alan for help. He and his father were choking with laughter, and unable to speak.

She ignored them and sighed. "Eva," she confided, "that's ze bride... nearly a lawyer already. Her new husband – in ze shmatte business," she winked, "Oy vey! A meshuggener, but gelt." She rolled her eyes, rubbed her fingers together and shrugged her shoulders. "Eva, she tells me we must be twisted at this shindig."

Alan found enough breath to enlighten me. "Bobeshi, I've told you a dozen times, it's *twisting,*" he emphasised. "Eva is determined to have us all to do *The Twist*!" And he demonstrated the latest craze for his grandmother's benefit.

Esther clapped her hands to her cheeks. "Oy vey, with *my* hips? You will pay ze doctor's bills, heh, Aaron, heh?" She watched his antics more closely, "Aaron! You schlemiel. You just like Zaydeh, God rest his soul. Move your tukhus." She grabbed my arm, "Show me Sarah, come. Show me twisted."

Not *quite* on the same wavelength then! My hackles collapsed with relief. At last, something to laugh about. I happily, and gratefully, joined in.

Esther was tiny and no more than six stone, I reckoned. She was a wrinkled, white-haired, elderly looking lady, though probably only in her 60s. She had a definite glint in her eye. There was no doubt who ruled this roost! A true Yiddishe Mama.

Esther's eyebrows knitted in concentration. Her knees began to move, then her feet, and eventually her hips.

"You got it, Mama," cried Benjamin, "you got it."

So, there we were, at the wedding. We had 'twisted the night away'. But now tradition reigned. Alan was in fine voice and led the singing, "*Hava Nagila, Hava Nagila... Hava Nagila, ve-nis mecha.*"

Esther glowed with pride as she joined her handsome grandson. Her darlink Aaron. She was so, so desperate for the next wedding to be his. Yes, there would be lots of tears. It would break her heart when, if ever, he eventually got round to telling her he was gay.

Glossary

Bobeshi	The more affectionate term for Grandmother
Bubbe	Grandmother - formal
Bubela	Baby
Chutzpah	Nerve, guts, daring
Gelt	Money
Goy	A Gentile, a non-jew
Hora	Dance
Kosher	Correct according to Jewish law
Latkes	Potato pancakes
Mazel Tov	Good luck / Congratulations
Meshuggener	Crazy man
Mossad	Israeli organisation for intelligence and special ops
Motek	Sweet one
Nu	A general term for – So? Well? Huh?
Oy vey	Exclamation of exasperation/dismay/grief
Schlemiel	Awkward
Shabbas	Sabbath
Shalom	Peace (usually when saying hello or goodbye)
Shickered	Drunk
Shmatte	Rag (shmatte business = rag trade)
Tukhus	Buttocks, bottom
Yamulke	Skull cap
Yiddishe Mama	A (very) Jewish mother
Zaydeh	Grandfather

Neil Robinson

Neil joined the writers' group almost three years ago and has so far published two books through Amazon: *Why Christians Don't Do What Jesus Tells Them To ...And What They Believe Instead* in 2012 and the contrasting *Short & Curly*, a selection of short stories in 2013.

Neil is a former English lecturer at a local university, and prior to that was a primary school headteacher for many years. His story 'Black And White And Read All Over' was written for the National Association of Writers' Groups' annual competition in 2014, and won first prize in the 'Short Story With A Given Phrase' category. The phrase in question was 'Was that a badger I just hit?'

Black And White And Red All Over

"Was that a badger I just hit?" Will Broxford exclaimed, bringing his car to a juddering halt. He was, he admitted reluctantly to himself, more concerned about possible damage to his new Corolla than to any animal that was unfortunate enough to have crossed his path in the moonlight. He got out of the car, surprised at how much his legs were shaking, and checked it for dents and scrapes. To his relief he could find none, though he couldn't be completely certain in the dark and would need to inspect it more thoroughly once he reached home.

Levering himself back into the vehicle, he was suddenly overcome with a compunction - maybe it was compassion - to go back along the road to find the badger, or whatever it was he had hit, to see if it was still there. Quite what he would do if it needed putting out of its misery, he wasn't sure. He couldn't see himself wringing its neck or bashing it over the head with a shovel, particularly as he hadn't got a shovel with him. It was a cold night, with a clear star-lit sky and a full moon, and he reached over to the passenger seat for his scarf; the new black and white one he'd been given at Christmas, though for the life of him he couldn't remember who by. He wrapped it round his neck, thinking how appropriate it was for a badger hunt, and banged the car door shut.

It always surprised him how long it took a vehicle to stop once you'd hit the brakes. There was, he could now see, something on the road a good couple of hundred yards back and he set off at a pace towards it. He turned over the events of the evening prior to this mishap; his meeting with his board of governors to discuss the school's imminent inspection, the confidence expressed in him, and the drink - just the one; a small whiskey - in the pub afterwards with his chair of governors. He was feeling trepidatious, naturally - there was nothing black and white about Ofsted - but also strangely buoyant, and not just because of the whiskey.

He reached the part of the road where he'd seen the shape on the road. There was a patch of dark, russet-coloured blood across the tarmac at his feet, sparkling in captured moonlight. The body of whatever creature it was lay half on the road, half against the grass verge. He could see now that it was too big to be a badger; more like a red deer. But its colouring was wrong for a deer; black with a flash of white. He was about to kneel down for a closer look when some movement on the road ahead caught his eye. He looked back the way he'd just come, towards his car and blanched. Its interior light was on. He hadn't, he knew, left it like that and he was certain he'd shut the door, slammed it even; there was no reason for the light to be on. "Just the moonlight," he told himself, "lighting up the inside." But it didn't look like moonlight. It was yellow, artificial.

And then he thought he could see movement in the car. Someone in the driver's seat, a head behind the headrest. He scrabbled in his coat pocket for the keys. "Damn you. You bloody idiot!" he chided himself. He'd left them in the ignition. He set off running, back towards the car, when he heard sirens behind him and, turning, saw in the distance the flashing lights of a police car and ambulance. The police would help him; he wouldn't have to confront whoever was in his car alone. But as they cleared the bend, he was overcome with nauseous dread. None of this was making any sense. Who, he wondered, had called the police, the ambulance? And why would they respond for just a badger or a deer? And then something, some intuition, prompted him to look back at his car.

It was no longer there.

The police car and ambulance had stopped, blocking the road behind them, and officers and paramedics were standing over the heap on the ground. Will called out to them, pointing frantically to where his car should have been. "So glad you're here," he said. "Someone's just stolen my car." The policeman looked at him disdainfully, almost as if he wasn't there, and carried on talking to one of the paramedics.

"Did you hear what I said?" Will shouted, losing control. "My car's been stolen, not five minutes ago. You have to do something."

"I'll call it in," the police officer said, pulling his radio out of his pocket.

"Thank you," Will said. That was something at least.

"White Corolla," the officer said, "one occupant, white male, dead at the scene."

"What?" Will stammered. "What are you talking about? Of course he's not dead. He's gone off in my car."

"Wrapped it round a telegraph pole," the policeman continued. "Went clean through the windscreen... No seatbelt... Death not immediate, no... Looks like he was able to make the call himself. God knows how, the state of him. Poor bugger."

Will felt his legs buckle. There was his car, not three feet away, the front sliced in two by a telegraph pole. Why had he not seen it before now? And how had it got back here? He sank to the ground, next to the body in the road. A face he recognised stared back at him with glassy eyes, its skull crushed flat against the tarmac, like broken eggshell. The hand that had obscured the face from above still held a mobile phone.

As the last of his consciousness slipped away, Will caught sight of the badger lying clipped and broken in the undergrowth.

Or perhaps it was nothing more than a bloodied, black and white scarf.

The Clock Struck One

I step up on to the bus for a journey I've taken so many times before. Usually it takes about twenty minutes to get into town, but I know that today it'll take much longer. I'm going to see my father.

The birthday card came out of the blue. It arrived on my birthday, of course, so it wasn't out of the blue in that sense, but it was the first I'd ever had off my dad. It was the first he'd ever sent. In it he'd written, "If you'd like to meet, please call me," with his number.

She must have the card by now. I timed it to arrive for her birthday and even if it didn't get delivered on time it must be there now. I know I hardly deserve a response, but I'd so much like one. Need one. Even if it's to tell me to get lost. I'd understand it if that's how she felt.

I didn't reply. Not at first anyway. Then I texted him and told him I would meet him. He texted back almost straight away with a picture of himself. I wouldn't have recognised him. He left my mum and me just after I was born.

I didn't send him a picture of me.

No photo, but at least she's prepared to meet me. More than I hoped for really. Thank God for the Internet. I'd never have found her otherwise.

I sit on one of the seats facing into the bus. I don't want to look out of the window. I read his instructions again: meet @ the café in market square @ 12. please wait for me. I've a long way to drive. looking 4ward 2 seeing u after all this time, dad x x

I haven't told mum I'm meeting him.

Hold-ups on the A66. I left enough time and now I'm going to be late. She might not wait. Wouldn't blame her. I'm hardly the most reliable person in her life. Pray to God she will. Text her to ask her to.

After an eternity, the bus lurches to a halt. I put up my brolly and walk through the rain to the café. I buy a decaffeinated coffee and sit at a table in the corner. I'm early but it isn't long before he's late. Another text: held up in traffic please wait.

Finally. I made it. Parking took ages too. I pull my coat round me and run to the café, nearly an hour late. Good job there, Tom, that's the way to treat her. The place is half empty. I scan the faces, looking for some who looks like me, or Katherine, but no-one holds my gaze. Which of them is she?

I know it's him as soon as he walks into the café. He looks much older than I thought he would. He glances round, surveying faces, but has no way of recognising me. He sits down at the table in the window and looks out. I look away, just in case. I step back and watch him from across the street, secure in the shadows. I feel sorry for him.

She's gone. Who can blame her. I blew it. Again.

The return bus comes into view and I step up to the bus stop. This was a big mistake and I want to be at home, with mum. Thirty-two years is a long time not to know someone. Not to know your own dad. The bus stops and when everyone is on board, pulls away again.

As the clock strikes one, I cross the road and push open the door of the café.

Pillar Of Salt

At 50, Tom Fletcher had reached a sort of crossroads in his life. No, not a crossroads, a dead end. The feeling that had haunted him for most of his adult life emerged from the shadows to take up noisy residence in his head. It did not make for a particularly happy birthday. How could it when he felt he had wasted those 50 years? He really didn't like his life. Superficially, he was successful; he was a businessman and company director; he had a presentable wife, two reasonably stable children and a large house in what was known locally as a highly desirable area.

He knew he had to do something. He couldn't stay with Joyce; that the house was highly desirable while she no longer was, was an irony that was not lost on him. It wasn't so much that they'd drifted apart but that, at some unspecified time in the past, they had each jumped into separate vehicles and had hurtled off in different directions.

He needed a solution, if one were possible, that did not entail solicitors, law courts and tearing apart everything he'd ever worked for. The kids were more or less independent now and he'd been a hopeless parent anyway. While most of their upbringing had fallen to him, he always had the feeling he'd let them down and should never have been a father. Someone should have told him, back when Joyce started insisting it was time to start a family, "No, not you, mate. You'll be lousy at it." But they hadn't and instead he and Joyce had had two children in quick succession; babies she seemed to lose interest in once they stopped being babies. But he was becoming bitter, and he didn't want to be. What he wanted was some way of putting things right; for himself, mainly - he acknowledged that - but also for the kids.

If anyone could return to an earlier time in life simply by willing it, it would be Tom. His thoughts were perpetually occupied with the idea that if he could find some way of returning to, say, the months leading up to his marriage, in the late nineteen-seventies, he'd be able to set things right and correct all his mistakes, second time around. He wouldn't marry Joyce, that's for sure, wouldn't pin himself down to marriage at all, not until much later anyway. Everyone had said they'd been too young at the time. Of course, this would mean Daniel and Penny wouldn't exist, at least not in their current form, but Tom was pretty sure they'd be around with half the genetic complement they had now - their mother's – with someone else providing the other half; the man she'd marry instead of him. It was an absolute certainty she'd find someone else, and that she would have children with him. She had been the driving force behind their marrying as well as their becoming parents; that wouldn't change. Who knows, maybe she'd have *more* children with another man. Maybe the third or fourth child that Tom had denied existence when he'd had his vasectomy, would see the light of day in the new reality he envisaged. And, with a bit more luck, maybe all of them would find themselves with a better father than he had been.

What would happen to the reality he intended leaving behind? The one where none of this had occurred - the unhappy marriage, the failings as a parent? Perhaps it would cease to be entirely, like a cauterised artery. Or maybe he'd just be found dead in his bed and the rest of it would go as normal, or...

But he couldn't think too deeply about what was going to happen to the present here and now. He'd just have to leave that to fate, or God, or whatever it was that was in charge of such things; the same controlling force that was going to grant him, he felt sure, special dispensation to take another crack at it. With this conviction, his wishful thinking intensified. On this his birthday, he would will himself back to that easier time and start again.

At first it felt like mild vertigo, a dizzy spell that took him by surprise and caused him to lose his balance. He slumped in his office chair and closed his eyes. He gripped the arms of the chair but then realised that this might give the wrong impression to whatever cosmic force was now taking charge of him - that he wanted to cling on to the present - so he let go and allowed it to lift him out of his body.

Once he started to fall, he fell rapidly.

Back beyond the day in September that changed everything, back before his own promotion. Before hysteria over the royal death, before his first breakdown (how strange that feels in reverse); the kids leaving home, past the difficult move to the new house and, eventually, out of the digital age.

...Into the callous eighties, when he made his money, which, with an unexpected relief, he now feels falling away; his children becoming ever younger, ever more demanding, until finally they vanish.

He feels himself falling further, back into an even more primitive age. The nineteen-seventies, where he's young again and slimmer, both physically and mentally, all of the accrued wisdom of his years, which he hardly ever noticed he had, stripped away somewhere in his backward flight. It is, he thinks, a small price to pay, especially now that he feels his body returned to its twenty-something state that pleases and re-invigorates him. His burning ambition has returned too, along with all of his worries about 'making it' and supporting his young wife and the family she wants... and of failure. But it doesn't matter; he will deal with all of that much better this time. He won't have a young wife or children waiting in the wings; he'll know how to marshal his anxieties and use them productively. Enough of his old self will survive to guide him through that. He'll reassure his younger self that all will be well.

He can, he suddenly realises, become a gambling man and with his future knowledge make his fortune betting on the outcomes of

Cup Finals and Grand Nationals and even Christmas number ones. With a little application, he'll be able to recall all of these and decides he'll write them down as soon as he arrives at his destination, in case they fade from his mind over time. He feels a frisson of excitement at the success he is going to make of everything this time round.

He becomes aware, as he hurtles through the vortex, that he isn't slowing down. He is going to have to jump, to disembark from his backward journey at some point soon. It's the early days of his marriage, and a sense of the elation he'd felt then catches him by surprise. He'd forgotten it, smothered as it has been by all the later complications. He braces himself as he experiences, in reverse of course, his own wedding, sensing again his uncertainty and lack of conviction. But it doesn't matter, the mistake is being undone.

Then courting, as his mother always called it - old fashioned even then – when he is free and life enjoyable, though, knowing what lies ahead, also uncomfortably ominous. He will jump any time now, even though he is aware he's travelling faster than ever, deeper into his own past. He braces himself; he's reached a point before he's even met Joyce. This is further than he intended to go but it will do; his teenage years, unlike his childhood, were happy. He has no objection to experiencing them again. So he tells himself to jump. But jumping, he now realises, was only a metaphor. He can no more jump than he can stop to blow his nose; this is a metaphysical experience where legs and noses are an illusion, physical attributes that will only return when the ride ends and he surfaces again in his own younger body. So he wills himself to stop instead, like he used to will himself to wake up from bad dreams, but instead he just keeps falling.

He's a boy now. Young Tommy. Alone, feeling the abandonment and anguish of his father's leaving. Grief, as he now recognises it. The shiny kernel that should be at the heart of this younger self is dented and dull. His older self makes to touch it, to give the young boy comfort and consolation, but it remains out of reach. He cries, experiencing the pain all over again, until he collides with the moment he learnt of his dad's death, the single event that wrenched the life from him and closed down everything that was warm and bright.

Then beyond. His daddy alive again, lifting him onto his shoulders, the thing at the centre of him bright and shiny once more. He wants to live here, in this one moment, forever, with time stopped, prevented from travelling forward again.

But he keeps on falling backwards, further back into the past of his own life. To where he's happy, with mummy and daddy near, and nothing to worry about. He doesn't even know what worrying is any more. The big dog next door sometimes frightens him but once his mummy comes out in her sunny pinny and he can wrap his arms around her legs. He is happy again even if everything is silly because it's all back to front.

The smell of milk. That is all there is to him now. He smells of it, he wants it. He is warm. Words have failed him; he has no words.

They have gone. They have not arrived yet. Smells and feeling warm or cold or hungry or messy. That is all. A little world of his own little body.

Then he's back where it's dark and red, wet and warm. There's noise; steady and loud. Nice noise. And he feels a sense of unravelling, of everything coming apart, unknitting. Anything that might be considered consciousness - his consciousness – is obliterated.

He is a string of nucleotides, but he doesn't know it. Doesn't know anything. He is a strand of RNA in search of another strand of RNA; he is a chemical half.

And then he is nothing at all. The strands that once made him are absorbed back into the bodies from which they came.

Everything about him has gone.

And time lurches forward again. Another string of nucleotides, not his, finds its way in the dark to one that waits for it.

And another child is born, another grows up with his mummy and daddy. There is no accident this time because the new child is ill the day his dad should travel and he stays at home instead. Another child, still whole and happy, goes to his school in his place and, later, finds true love where he didn't.

Another has a successful career and raises a child - just the one - instead of him. She doesn't know, this other, that hers is an alternative life, one that might never have been and was never intended to be.

In some other reality, Tom lay slumped in his chair. His body was still warm, and his heart beat rapidly, but he was not there.

He had had his birthday wish, his second chance to begin all over again.

Hayley Cordley

Hayley was born in Dumfries and grew up in Gretna. She has been writing since she was a young child, inspired by English assignments at school. Even though these stories were meant to be brief, she found it hard to stop once she started writing.

She published her first crime novel, *Brandon & Bailey,* in 2013. Knowing that she couldn't stop at one novel, she is now working on a series about the same characters. She has also been working on short stories, novellas, scripts and poems, and finds inspiration in everyday events.

A Moment In Time

It had been several years since my last case. I had remained hidden away in the manor, with only Mrs Hopeland, my maid, for company. I was beginning to wonder if I was losing my touch; cases had always had their way of finding me, not the other way around.

I heard the doorbell ring from my office. I didn't get many visitors and when I did, it was mainly people I was trying to avoid. Before I had the chance to return to my book I heard a voice. A woman's voice. I slowly closed the book and listened.

"Good evening. Pardon my intrusion but I am in need of assistance," the woman said. "Is this the home of Mr. Braithwood?"

"It is indeed, my dear." Mrs Hopeland replied, "Come in. I'll see if he's about." I heard the woman enter the drawing room as Mrs Hopeland came up the stairs. She knocked gently on my office door.

"Mr Braithwood, sir, there is a young woman here to see you."

"Bear with me, Mrs Hopeland," I replied, slotting the book back into the bookcase. "I will be down in a few minutes."

"Very good, sir. I'll get some tea for our guest," she said.

I listened as Mrs Hopeland made her way back downstairs and into the kitchen. I looked across the room at my reflection in the window and straightened out my tie before getting to my feet. It'd been three days since I had left the office and two days since I had left that chair and my back was aching more than ever. Unable to take my eyes from the window, I sighed. What had become of my life? My career was more of a hobby than a job. I'm not part of a police force, I work alone. I solve cases long before the police have even uncovered their first clue. It is a curse I have been burdened with and something I must live with for the rest of my life.

Slowly I dragged myself across the room and towards the door, uncertain of whether to meet this woman or not. I pushed open the door and stepped out onto the landing. The air was cold and still. I peered over the banister; a dim light shone from the drawing room, and I could see the silhouettes of Mrs Hopeland and the unknown woman on the wall. From what I could see, she was a slender woman, wearing some kind of feathery headwear. I was instantly intrigued. I slowly wandered down the staircase and across the hall to the drawing room before giving two soft knocks on the door to instruct, Mrs Hopeland's cue to leave the room.

She walked past me, her head low. "Is there something bothering you, Mrs Hopeland?" I asked but as I expected she didn't reply and carried on walking back into the kitchen. Concerned, I stepped into the drawing room and quietly closed the door behind me. The young woman sat in the leather armchair beside the fireplace, sipping the tea that Mrs Hopeland had offered her.

"Mr Braithwood?" she said in a hushed tone.

"Is there something I can help you with, madam?" I asked.

"Oh, yes sir," she said, "I am in need of your assistance. You see, my daughter is missing and the police have called off the search. You are my last hope. I have heard so much about you. If you were to help me, I would be forever in you debt."

"What is your name, madam?" I asked.

"Mrs Ashgrave" she replied. "Olivia Ashgrave."

"Well, Mrs Ashgrave, how much are you willing to pay?" I asked.

"Pay?" Mrs Ashgrave said. "Sir, I have very little money. I have been unable to work since Molly's disappearance."

"Madam," I said, cutting her off. "What kind of man would I be, if I were to take money from a lady in search of her child? I was merely enquiring to determine how much assistance you are willing to provide. I will help you, but I will need your help. After all, how am I to know what your daughter looks like?"

"In any way I can, sir," Mrs Ashgrave replied instantly.

"Excellent. In that case, you will stay here and we shall start the case in the morning. Mrs Hopeland will get you a change of clothes and something to eat. There is a spare bedroom in the left wing, which you can use," I said. "Don't let this dwell on your mind too much, my dear. I will make it my duty to find your daughter, alive and well," I reassured the distressed mother.

"Thank you, sir," she replied. "I could not be more grateful."

"I will see you in the morning, Mrs Ashgrave. If you need anything, Mrs Hopeland will help you," I said with a smile, before heading back towards the entrance of the drawing room. I slowly pulled the door shut until it was closed fully.

When I looked back into the main hall, Mrs Hopeland was awaiting my return with her arms filled with bed sheets and pillowcases.

"You have a good heart, sir," she said.

"I am doing what any other civilised human being would do, Mrs Hopeland," I sighed. "Having a good heart has nothing to do with this situation."

Although I had dismissed Mrs Hopeland's comment, something inside me stirred, something I had never felt before. For that moment in time - a mere second - I knew I was doing the right thing.

The Fifth Case

Years passed. Memories faded.

Time ran out. The future came.

I'd give the world for us to be together again.

I hope you do the same.

I can feel my world stop spinning,

and my life coming to an end.

Nothing lasts forever,

except for this love I send.

There was no need to be afraid.

I had returned to set you free.

You didn't listen.

You were frightened and tried to flee.

You were the kindest, most generous person I'd ever met;

I just thought I'd let you know.

Although none of that matters now.

I guess it was just my time to go.

Do you remember me?

Of course you do.

My name is Jason Chase.

I was your fifth and final case...

Brandon & Bailey

Brandon & Bailey are police officers who work in the small town of Holston. Hayley is writing a series of books about them, the first of which was published in 2013. This extract is from chapter two of that book, where the team come across the first of a series of murders by what turns out to be a cunning serial killer.

Dylan scampered up the stairs with all of his equipment packed into several cases. Brandon and I met him at the top of the steps to grab some of them from his aching arms. Tom had already been to the car park at the rear of the building, and brought the van around to collect us. With everything now piled into the back of it, we hopped in and slid the door shut.

"Where exactly is this body, Jenna?" asked Devon, fastening his seatbelt.

"It's in that forest near the Zodiac Hotel," she replied as she started up the van and left the police station with the sirens blaring.

A long and silent fifteen minutes later, we arrived at the site where the body had been found. Inspector Todd Finch from the forensics department stood awaiting our arrival.

"Good morning, Inspector," said Devon, as he approached him.

"Morning," yawned Todd. "Follow me."

As we walked through the forest behind the inspector, I listened to the sounds around us. Sirens, clicks from camera shutters and zips from evidence bags; not the usual sounds you would expect to hear in a forest. Trying to keep up with Todd, I looked at Brandon; although we were walking to a potential crime scene, he still had a smile on his face.

Soon we arrived at the scene. In a ditch-like area lay the body of a sheep, which confused me slightly. If we were here to investigate a body, I thought it would at least be a human body.

"That's a sheep," I pointed out.

"Yes, we aware of that, Bailey," said Dylan, opening one of his many cases.

"We're here to examine a sheep carcase?" I asked.

"No, of course not," he said with a sigh of annoyance. He cut some of the wool away from the animal with a sharp metal device. "Quite an extraordinary idea, don't you think?"

"What? Finding a dead sheep," I asked.

"No," he sighed again. "By placing a human corpse within an animal's body, both bodies will decompose together at the same time. Poor bugger was butchered up to fit inside the animal."

"Wait a minute! What are you saying? That there's a body inside that animal?" I gasped.

I had to admit it was a clever idea, but not clever enough, I guess. Dylan removed a few bones from the ribcage of the beast before placing them into multiple evidence bags. As he peeled back the flesh of the animal, he revealed the victim's face. The smell was putrid, and the sight of the man wasn't pleasant either. I backed away and stood beside Devon who was white in the face, and rendered completely speechless by this discovery.

The unfortunate man must have been about forty. He was dressed in a black suit, and wore a plain gold ring on his left ring finger. As Dylan removed more and more of the sheep's flesh, the majority of the body was revealed. Attached to his body was a badge, held on with a golden pocket clip. The badge was from the Zodiac Hotel. I recognised the logo immediately. An elegant silver font in the centre of the badge showed the victim's name was Keith Hepson.

As the sickly feeling died away, I knelt down beside Dylan again. As I did so, I noticed a few small crimson flakes around the evidence bags which were resting against his knee. He noticed me staring at them as he looked up from his work.

"I collected a few of those flakes," he said. "I'll be able to find out what they are, as soon as we get back to the station."

"I don't think it will take much to figure out what they are," I said, placing my finger on top of one of the many flakes. When I managed to make it stick to my skin, I rubbed it between my thumb and index finger, breaking it into pieces and leaving a red smudge on my fingertips.

"It's paint."

Michelle Naish

Michelle has been a member of the writers' group for three years. She enjoys the friendly encouragement she gets from other members. She loves to write poems and short stories.

Michelle was born in Carlisle where she worked in a nursery for twenty-one years, as well as in factories.

The Poppy

In Flanders fields
The poppies grow,
Where a gentle breeze
Catches them so.

The poppy, so bright and red,
That we all wear with such pride
On each and every
Remembrance Day.

The poppy, a symbol
For all the fallen forces,
Men and women,
Past and present.
It is so right
That we should always
Remember them.

What You See Is What You Get

Sitting talking with some friends the other day,

One of them turns to me and says,

"You say some true and powerful things

When it comes to the meaning of life."

"Oh yeah, that's me!" I say out loud,

When deep down inside what I really

Want to say is, "Don't sit there

And patronise me

Then go behind my back

And criticise me."

Because what you see is what you get,

And you may not like it

But that's okay with me,

Because I am me and that's how I'll stay.

Quick! Look Behind You

We had been in China for just over a week and were going to visit the Wolong Panda Reserve in the mountains.

"It's going to be a long day," our tour guide tells us. "It will take us four hours to get there. But we will see some lovely sights while we are travelling."

When we eventually arrive at the panda reserve we are told that most of the pandas staying in the reserve have been raised there. Some of them share their enclosures while others have their own.

As we walk around outside the pandas' enclosure I notice that there is a large courtyard for the pandas. They can climb the trees provided or just laze around in the sun eating bamboo. This too is provided for them. We are told that we can go inside the panda enclosure but we must be very quiet.

I can't wait to go in. I turn to Sheila and say, "I hope we see some pandas after such a long trip."

Once inside the enclosure, we don't spot any pandas. After strolling round the enclosure for ten minutes we still haven't seen anything and I am starting to become deflated; we have come all this way and not seen a single panda. So I slowly walk over and sit down despondently on one of the benches in the enclosure.

"Quick! Look behind you!" Sheila says slowly. I turn around and see a lovely baby panda creeping up behind me. I just stare in amazement at this beautiful animal. The panda stops walking, looks at me, climbs up onto the bench and sits down beside me.

I just can't believe what is happening. The cub looks at me once again then places its paw onto my knee. I can't speak so I just look at Sheila and point at the panda. Sheila nods, gives me the thumbs-up and takes some photos. I slowly put my arm around the panda and it moves a bit closer, putting its head on my shoulder.

When it eventually gets down, it walks back over to the entrance of its indoor enclosure. Before going back inside it turns around and looks at me again. My heart just melts.

I walk back towards Sheila telling her I can't believe what has happened.

"Neither can I," she says. "I'm so pleased I got some good photos otherwise I'm not sure anyone would believe us when we got home!"

Norma Mainwaring

Norma joined the Carlisle Writers' Group in the autumn of 2013. She enjoys the discipline of producing a new story for each meeting.

She is also a member of a reading group, and records for the Talking Newspaper.

Norma recently celebrated her Golden Wedding and has two married daughters.

A Moment In Time

Reg turned his face skyward as the familiar sound of the Merlin engine reached his ears. His old heart skipped a beat as the Spitfire passed over his head and executed a perfect roll, the sun catching the wingtips and turning them to silver.

Until the year she died, Martha and he had had been coming to the air show for years. After a while, Reg started coming alone.

"How long ago was that?" Like so many things nowadays, Reg couldn't remember. He only realised that he had turned ninety this month when his son reminded him. He had tried often over the years to recall all those young men who had died in that far-off summer of 1940 but they remained in the shadows. So many times he had asked God, "Why me? Why am I still alive when all those brave young men died?" He had never had an answer. How many of them had Reg seen spiralling down to the earth, and heard the screams of those consumed by fire? It still haunted his dreams.

Nowadays, he tried to think of the happier times. The noisy nights in the local pub and the dances in the Mess, where he had met a lovely young WAAF called Martha.

Reg realised that he must have been walking for quite a while lost in thought, as suddenly there was a Spitfire parked in front of him, as if proudly waiting for the call of 'Scramble' that would never come again. As he passed slowly under the wing, he felt the residual heat from the engine and heard the familiar tick-tick as it cooled down. His mind flooded with memories as the smell of fuel oil and old leather washed over him in waves. His heart began to flutter wildly, and somewhere he thought he could hear a clanging bell.

*　　　*　　　*　　　*　　　*

Reg was running, the loose strap of his flying helmet flapping beneath his chin. The bell had stopped now, but he could still hear the echo bouncing around inside his skull. The adrenalin rushed through his body, accompanied by a dry mouth and familiar sick feeling in the pit of his stomach. With one graceful movement he stepped onto the wing and slid into the cockpit, his eyes automatically checking the array of dials before him. Hands reached in and helped him shrug into his safety harness. He inhaled the familiar rubber smell of his oxygen mask lying on his chest, and heard "Good luck, sir!" as he pressed the starter button.

Feet on the rudder, he taxied across the grass, and as he gathered speed, Reg leaned back into his seat feeling the reassuring pressure of the 'chute against his spine. He exchanged a thumbs-up with the pilots on either side of him, then reached up pulling the canopy shut, trapping inside the smell of grass and new-mown hay. As he slowly pulled the joystick towards himself, the plane left the ground. Seconds later, he heard the dull thud of the wheels retract beneath him.

Now the men were no longer shadows. Now they were all around him. All young, and untouched by time. In graceful symmetry the Spitfires climbed, their noses pointing into the perfect blue of an English summer day, flying to victory and captured for ever in a moment in time.

*   *   *   *   *

The pilot found Reg lying on the grass, under the wing, his eyes still open. As he told them later in the Mess, "It might have been a trick of the light, but I could swear the old man was smiling."

Highland Getaway

They were sitting in the pub garden, the map spread out before them like a multi-coloured tablecloth. Charlotte had lost count of how many times it had been unfolded since they arrived at the Stag Inn. Every detail of each daily walk was marked out to the nth degree. No wonder she had ceased to enjoy them! Thankfully, the holiday was nearly over, and she would be able to relax on her own, with her feet up.

"Do I really mean that?" Charlotte thought. After all, she *had* enjoyed being with Stuart when they first met, but the relentless timetable that he had mapped out for the week was the last straw. Even at the end of the day, they had to have an after-dinner stroll, followed by a nightcap before she fell exhausted into bed.

Charlotte realised now that Stuart had been a control freak from the start. At first it had felt like cosseting; however, as time went by, the constant adhering to his plans paled. No spontaneity and consequently, no enjoyment. My God, even on arrival, he had marched her to the nearest outdoor shop, insisting she needed a new anorak and boots! Since then, she had just wanted it all to be over.

They had met just three months before, when Stuart had literally bowled her over on Princes Street. She should have seen the signs then when, after apologising profusely and assuring himself that she wasn't hurt, he had hurried her into a nearby shop and insisted on replacing her torn woollen gloves with a very expensive leather pair. He then escorted her to *The Scotsman* for tea and scones.

After introducing themselves (Stuart Sinclair architect, Charlotte Taylor accountant), she explained she was visiting Edinburgh only for the day from Carlisle, so of course he escorted her to the train, and before it departed they had exchanged business cards. She knew *now* that she should have seen the pattern of things but when, a week later, an invitation to a weekend in Edinburgh had come, she had accepted. After all, he was tall, blond and handsome, so what was there not to like?

As time went on, Charlotte got used to Stuart arranging everything. He booked his own hotel on visits to Carlisle, and on arrival would present the programme for the weekend to her.

And now, sitting here surrounded by the beauty of the Scottish Highlands, Charlotte knew the relationship was at an end. She turned to Stuart and said, "I'm sorry, but I've forgotten something." She jumped to her feet and hurried inside the hotel before he could reply. At the reception desk, she asked for a taxi right away to meet her round the side of the building. Then, she bounded up the stairs to her room and in ten minutes was packed and looking over the banister at Stuart pacing in the hall below.

She rushed down the back stairs and through the kitchen, ignoring the surprised looks of the staff. The taxi barely had time to pull up round the corner before Charlotte hurled herself and her cases onto the back seat, slamming the door behind her.

"My! You're in a hurry, lassie!" exclaimed the driver.

Pausing only to catch her breath, she said, "Take me to the nearest station, please!"

As the taxi drew away from the hotel, she had a glimpse through the window of Stuart in conversation with the receptionist.

At the station, the driver said, "That'll be seven pounds, lassie."

"Keep the change!" said Charlotte with a smile, placing her last Scottish notes onto his outstretched palm.

The Clock Struck One

"Welcome to Chicago!"

A nice woman with a beaming smile greets us as we enquire where to get transport to our hotel.

It's 2nd June 2005, and we have just made our first footprints on American soil. A long walk from the plane, and we join one of the many queues in security. Gradually, we arrive at the desk and hand over our passports, green cards and customs declarations, to a stern-faced woman complete with side-arm.

"Press your index finger on the pad."

"Sorry, is this right?" I say as I comply. "I'm still a bit deaf from the flight."

The stern face suddenly breaks into a smile.

"Don't worry, honey, you're doing fine!"

That's it! We have officially arrived. Hauling our cases, we present ourselves at the transport stop. We are greeted by the driver who puts our luggage in... the trunk. We are in America now! We join the people already on the bus and settle down. The driver returns about ten minutes later with a gallon of Coke and enough

French fries to feed a small country.

It takes us about twenty minutes to exit from the airport. O'Hare is very large. During this time, the driver is stuffing the French fries into his mouth between gulps of Coke. Fortunately, before we turn onto the freeway he has finished his snack, releasing both hands again to grasp the wheel. From then on, apart from the occasional burp, we make steady progress, and gradually the skyscrapers grow ever larger in the bus windows as we approach the city. We start dropping people at their hotels.

"Drop me at the Hancock Building!" a strident voice intones. This force-of-nature charges down to the front of the bus shouting over her shoulder, "Make sure you've got all the bags, Wendell, you know I can't carry anything!"

They leave the bus and the driver, muttering under his breath, pulls out into the traffic. After a few 'oohs' and 'aahs' at the sights, we are starting to flag. There are another two drops and the radio activates.

"The woman from the Hancock has left a luggage strap on the bus."

"What?" The driver throws both his hands in the air. "I hate that! I really hate it when they do that!"

As we swerve, his hands drop back onto the wheel, and a few minutes later we are dropped at our hotel. We claim our luggage from the trunk, and follow the bell-boy into the foyer. At the reception, one of the Stepford Wives greets us.

"Oh, you're English! Cool! Is this your first visit?"

As she takes our passports and does the paperwork, she doesn't notice she is dealing with two zombies! We get a high-speed lecture on the facilities, and then we exchange looks of relief as she summons the bell-boy.

A door at the back of Reception opens, and Colonel Sanders appears - apart from the lack of a Stetson, it's him, complete with pointy beard.

"I heard the English voices. I'm the manager, blah blah blah... I've been to England myself. Blah...blah."

At last, we are in the lift, down the corridor, into the bedroom, tip passed over and the doors shut. We make a quick cup of tea, and then collapse onto the beds. Alan starts to snore... and suddenly we are woken by voices in the corridor and it's two hours later. We unpack, shower and dress, and head back in Reception. We approach a young man at the concierge desk.

"Good evening, sir, ma'am. How can I help you?"

"Can you recommend a restaurant nearby?" we ask.

"You're English. Cool!"

He directs us to a restaurant five minutes away; Petterino's is a bar/restaurant. The walls are covered with dozens of caricatures of stars past and present, some more recognisable than others. We are shown to a table and a waitress with startling white teeth approaches.

"My name is Shana. Remember the film *Shane*? Well, my Mom just loved Alan Ladd. You're English aren't you?'" Etc, etc..

Alan orders a rib-eye steak and I have a fish platter. I have lost track of time but I realise that I am very hungry and the food is delicious. Shana is back at the table saying how nice Alan is to talk to. Well, she has to earn her tip somehow!

"How polite you Brits are!"

We are entertained by a couple at the next table. The husband is being harangued by his wife.

"You really don't know how to handle my mother, do you? I don't know what you were thinking of! You'd better send her flowers."

We are wilting again, so with effusive goodbyes we exit the restaurant and return to the hotel. In the distance, a clock strikes one. I try, and fail, to translate this into British time, and give up. We are in Chicago and our holiday is under way. We are quickly in bed, and I am asleep even before Alan starts snoring!

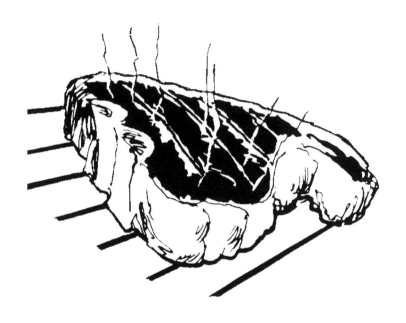

Janette Fisher

Janette has been a member of Carlisle Writers' Group for five years. Her poetry has been published in anthologies by Forward Press and in various magazines.

Her first anthology *There's Enough Blue in the Sky* will be published soon and she is currently writing her first novel, *The Re-invention of Jenny Wren*. Janette is the Administration Officer at a local project for adults with learning disabilities.

A widow since 2010, Janette lives in Carlisle and has two daughters.

A Clock Strikes Thirteen

Through the trees, they saw a light
As a haze over the village ahead,
And weary from walking many miles
Two travellers thought they might find a bed.

As they made their way to the village
A mist descended, cold and damp,
Hindering the travellers on their quest,
Shrouding light from both window and lamp.

Cloaked in the mist, the village was still,
With no sign of life to be seen.
The travellers made their way to the inn
As ahead in the distance, a clock struck thirteen.

As the last chime rang, from beyond the grave,
Ghosts of the dead filled the streets.
The travellers were frozen, unable to move
Fear and dread chilling their bones, head to feet.

Petrified they looked for a haven,
But no matter how hard they tried
There was nowhere for them to run to,
All possible routes of escape were denied.

Surrounded by the walking dead
And powerless in their plight,
They were quickly consumed by spectres
Who carried their souls off into the night.

Sated, the dead returned to their graves,
The clock once again struck thirteen,
And two piles of dust were all that remained
On the site where the travellers had been.

By The Running Water

I am eager to see my parents as I push open the large ornate gates that are a portal to our special place. The sun is shining brightly as always, and its glow highlights the astonishing beauty that befalls my eyes. In front of me are magnificent gardens filled with colour and aroma, from the masses of flowers and shrubs bedecked with a myriad of exquisite blooms. Standing majestically amongst the shrubbery are statues of various forms and here and there, a small topiary maze dots the landscape alongside formal water pools, giving the gardens the grandeur of Capability Brown.

Ahead of me in the distance, is the river, its running water integral to this serene vista. As I walk along the pathways towards it, I can't help but be soothed by the sound of water rippling over stones and small waterfalls coupled with birds singing in the trees and on the wing. I invariably visit this idyll when I am troubled and my heart always lightens as soon as I am here. Perhaps it's the scent from the flowers, perhaps it's the tranquillity of this place, but all the heaviness of my burdens seem to lift as soon as I enter the celestial entrance.

When I first started visiting this place, my parents would meet me at the gates and their being there for me was so reassuring. They would take me by the hand and lead me through the gardens until we reached our inner sanctum. But that was long ago; now they wait for me by the water and my footsteps quicken as I catch a glimpse of them in the distance, eager to have them beside me.

Following the path of the river, I walk quickly on and go through a dark tunnel which is carved into a stone embankment. Hieroglyphs decorate the main archway leading to an old bear pit, dark and dank, secluded from the sun. I stop for a second to let my eyes adjust to the darkness. It's cold and damp inside, with water dripping down the walls from the river running above. As I reach the stone staircase in the centre that leads out to the top level, I carefully climb the damp, moss-ridden steps leading back to the light. Emerging at the top, the sun is blinding and I have to shade my eyes for a while until they readjust to the light again. Then I walk on.

The running water is thunderous as the river falls, plunging into a lake. My parents come to meet me at the spot where we have met so many times before. As they take me in their arms in a comforting embrace, their love and presence fill my heart with so much happiness that I feel it will burst. All this reminds me how much I miss them when we are apart, making me cherish every moment that we spend here together.

The sun's rays are unbearably warm, the air humid and breathless, so we settle on the grass under a tree by the edge of the lake which looks so still and mirror-like today. Its surface is only disturbed only by the occasional ripple of a fish rising to feed and the foaming of a nearby waterfall. The sound of the rushing water creates a relaxing atmosphere, with birdsong and sounds from other creatures adding to the ambience. One can't help but feel at peace in such serene surroundings.

The shade from the tree is welcome as we sit talking, and as I tell my parents what is on my mind they listen intently as always. When I finish my recitation, they are happy to impart their advice and wisdom, a ritual we have gone through on many occasions over the years.

I haven't been with my parents long, when I hear a bell sound. Its ringing is a signal that it's time to leave. I'm reluctant to go, and turn a deaf ear in an attempt to steal a few more precious minutes with those I love so dearly. The bell sounds again, louder this time, and I know that I must go. I give my parents a farewell embrace, and retracing my steps along the river, quickly walk back to the pit, through the tunnel towards the gates, the bell getting louder every second. When I reach the gate, I turn and take one last look at this special place that I have come to rely on so much. I take heart in the knowledge that I will be back again in time.

I walk out of the gates, closing them behind me, the ringing almost deafening now. I turn, open my eyes and stretch out my hand to turn off my alarm disappointed to be woken from my slumber.

On rising, I'm ready to face a new day, the way ahead clear from the wisdom and advice gleaned from my parents. Although they passed on many years ago, they will always be there for me, by the running water, in my dreams.

A Mother's Love

From the very first time you hold your child,

Their first gift is your heart forever.

The love you give and they return

Is the bond that will hold you together.

Throughout their life, your love will be

A light that guides their way,

The beacon aglow in the darkness

Should they ever go astray.

Your love will give them courage

When the way ahead is unclear

And will give them strength, when needed

To help overcome their fear.

Your love will accept them, for who they are

Whatever they say or do.

Your love will forgive unreservedly

Because they are a part of you.

It's a love that will know no barriers,

Have no bounds, no expectations.

Your love will be unconditional,

Pure, with no complications,

A love that remains as constant

As the stars in the heaven above,

A gift no money on earth can buy

The gift of a mother's love.

Janet Patrick

Janet first came to the Writers' Group in June 2014 and enjoyed the experience of sharing work in a friendly, encouraging atmosphere.

Janet was born and brought up in Carlisle and over the years has worked in many different places, including offices, schools and factories. She loves nature, walking and drawing. She finds writing a way to create pictures with words that lead to telling stories.

White Horses

Heart in the sky,

Mane in the wind,

Flying the surf,

Coursing the blue,

We travel as one,

Here and gone.

Pounding, hammering, salt sharp breath,

Rush of blood and brine,

Crashing into silence,

Forever free.

Phoenix

Embers long dead,

Lost in reflection.

White ashes evoke Elizabethans,

Their faces powdered with bone.

Absurd at such a moment and yet,

Perhaps only in the grey dawn,

A life, as dust

Comes this movement from the hearth.

Hare

Tuned to the edge of the wind,
Standing like a man,
Nothing passes you by.

Nonchalant, something of a rake,
You are all loose limbs
And posturing.

Ready for flight in a second
Yet so languid,
Effortless you glide.

Touched by mist and moons,
Aching midsummer dances
In the secret dew.

A spirit free of time,
Caught in the half light,
You are gone.

Nigel Banks

Nigel made his first, dramatic appearance at the writers' group in 2014. Born in Bolton, Lancashire he has a background in theatre as both director and performer, as well as in teaching. A number of his plays have been broadcast, the most recent, *Borderline*, on Internet radio during July 2014.

Now happily retired, Nigel's his last post was as head of drama at Dover Girls' Grammar School. He lives near Brampton with his partner and their two labradors. When not involved in theatre or dog-walking, he supports lost causes: Bolton Wanderers F.C. and Lancashire Cricket Club.

Where Would They Sleep Tonight?

Hollow-eyed, sallow-skinned beneath the patina of street grime,
They shuffle towards their nightly resting place as dusk squats
Over the city and the evening revellers make merry.
No shielding cloud cover to cloak them from the searing chill
Under the bright stars pitiless gaze.

A day like any other standing on street-corners, mittened hands
Held out in hope as the uncaring crowds hurry past, eyes down.
Hostels, missions, and soup-kitchens – charity's dead hand
Has them clutched within the do-gooder's grasp.
No option but the gap-toothed grin of gratitude.
They get to know the havens of refuge: benches to lay their heads,

Cafes where a cuppa can last an hour looking at the rain,
Can't stay! It's on to the next port of call – library reading room to
slump
Over today's paper: celebrity scandal, fat-cat payouts, property
price-hike.
Headlines from a different world – different planet.

Once in a blue moon the Sally Army has a bed and hot meal
To keep body and soul together; the dirty old sheets, rank smell of
Unwashed bodies and rantings of alcohol-addled brains still
Beat standing all day down on Shacklewell Street while the rain
Hammers down and the cold seeps into the marrow.

Now they hove in sight of their chosen doorway dormitory only
To find a bed of studs – metal sentries guarding against unwanted
Invaders. A final nail in the coffin for these homeless pariahs.
They look up in despair to heaven for a merciful god to send
succour.
No answer: where would they sleep tonight?

A Lake District Day

The tarn edges the road to White Moss Common

Its water sludge-brown, dank and stagnant.

Flies meander over the surface; aimlessly

Purposeful in their secret mission,

They slalom among the fishing float reeds

To the accompaniment of a symphony –

A birdsong symphony of warbling, chittering,

Piping calls that affirm Life's pulse.

Only the keening cry of a peacock

Strikes a discordant note.

The fruitcake slab of fell, decorated green

Overlooks Rydal Water – an ink-blot shape

On the baize table-top of valley.

Puppet figures pause in their pottering.

One points a walking stick upwards at us.

Cattle and sheep browse undeterred by

The dull roar of traffic snaking its slow,

Relentless way along the side of the lake.

To the North the rolling vaults of hills

Are pierced by the headlong vapour trails

Of low-flying jets: the peace of the ancients

Pillaged by the obscene noise of war.

Over the lake other airborne craft are

Making their descent: black-headed gulls

Twitch in the air-currents, a heron skims

In to land on the water, while short-haul

Ducks speedboat at random.

We leave the Common and tread the Coffin Road

Back to Dove Cottage – a colourful band

Of mourners with no hearse to follow, just

Sandwiches cake and drink to draw us on.

A final detour through a wooded glade

Takes us to John's Grove, the familiar path

Used by William, Dorothy and brother John.

Pine-cones and twig detritus strew the well-

Worn steps of yesteryear.

If I Were In Prison, What Would I Be In For?

A hypothetical question, which I find difficult to address, because like the majority of the populace, I am an, upstanding, law-abiding member of the community. Not perfect by any means; guilty of various peccadilloes (I was recently found to have driven at 36mph in a 30mph zone and have to attend a Speed Awareness Course as a result), but never in danger of being sent to prison. Also like the majority of the populace I've been brought up to have a moral sense of Right and Wrong, to believe in fair-play, justice and the need for the Rule of Law in order for a liberal, democratic society to operate successfully. The system is far from perfect, as we know, but it works reasonably well much of the time. Where there are imperfections, inequalities, or downright incompetence there is usually some avenue that can be pursued to seek improvement or redress. We do not labour under the yoke of totalitarianism in this country, though some may argue that we have allowed ourselves to be at the mercy of global financial conglomerates, whose power now transcends that of our national or European governing bodies – but that's another story. I digress!

What set of circumstances could I envisage leading me to commit a crime, which would result in me having to serve a custodial sentence at Her Majesty's Pleasure? I can think of only two. The first is fairly predictable. Few of us can know what acts of violence we might be capable of unless confronted with an actual nightmare scenario. For example: an intruder breaks into your home at dead of night. You are woken by a noise, make your way downstairs to investigate and pick up an object with which to defend yourself. On discovering the intruder, you defend your property and your person with vigour, which results in the severe wounding, or even death, of the burglar. You are subsequently charged with using excessive force, and found guilty of manslaughter, but are given a comparatively light sentence because of the extenuating circumstances.

The other circumstance was suggested to me by a play I watched on television recently. Written by the award-winning dramatist Jimmy McGovern, it highlighted the anomalous legal principle of 'Joint Enterprise'. This law was first introduced in England in the 19th Century as a deterrent against the aristocracy's penchant for settling disputes by means of duelling. All those present at such events would find themselves charged with murder whether or not they actually wielded the sword, or fired the pistol. Now in the 21st century the police are using this archaic law as a weapon against gang violence. No longer do they have to prove that someone present during an assault was directly physically involved. If they did nothing to attempt to prevent the attack taking place, then they can be charged under the 'Joint Enterprise' principle. Predictably, this has led to several miscarriages of justice with innocent bystanders being charged and found guilty. A House of Commons Committee of Enquiry is going to look into this state of affairs, but that will be scant consolation to those innocents currently incarcerated (and their families). I could just about envisage a scenario in which I might be unwittingly witness to some crime, and not being the 'Gung-ho', 'Have-a-go' heroic type, I might well stand and watch horrified from the sidelines rather than wading in and trying to prevent the crime. Even in that unlikely set of circumstances, though, it's doubtful that I would be charged under the 'Joint Enterprise' law, as I don't tend to associate with felonious reprobates – at least, not to my knowledge!

Of one thing I am sure: if I were to be convicted of an offence and sent to prison, I would never survive the ordeal.

Susan Cartwright-Smith

Susan returned to Carlisle after an eventful career tailoring in the theatre, and joined Carlisle Writers' Group this year. She has previously produced stories to accompany puppet shows in Cumbria, and enjoys writing adult fairy tales, usually with a local slant.

She has two small boys to fill with wonder and mischief, and she takes part in extreme folk-dancing, having sustained more injuries in the last three years during clog and longsword dancing, than in the rest of her life.

Flood

That's all it is – stuff. And the floodline only came up to chest height here, so, you know, there is stuff that can be salvaged. Things above that height. I suppose I should be relieved that it was just… stuff.

So here I am, at the storage unit. The smell is dank, and it feels smaller and colder here. Colder than usual. I'm kind of dreading opening the door. Not because I expect a deluge to come flooding out, but because I don't know if I have the strength to unpack all this stuff, and make those trips to the skip outside.

The shriek of the door scraping across the floor echoes round the building and is louder than expected. The storage units are emptying, and strange echoes abound. The wardrobes, inherited from my great-uncle, his sharp cologne still ghosting the shelves, have a dark, silty tidemark, telling of their latest adventures. They have sported nearly eighty years of the very latest fashions, and are now wearing their shrouds. The blooms of bacteria adding nauseating colour to this grey box-room.

The bed I'd recently received as a house-warming present, still in its plastic wrapping, is leaning drunkedly against a sofa, sagging and soaking. The plastic served only to hold water, not hold it back. I grimly haul the mattress out to the skip, to join the rotting piles of other people's memories. Old diaries, letters, books with the corners of pages turned down, and loving inscriptions inside the front cover, wedding shoes, photo albums, a newspaper bought on the day of the birth of my first child – somehow I can't bear to throw them all in the skip. I can't really bear the thought of taking them home either, to try and dry them out, to try and save something of what they represent, as if not owning these possessions means the memories don't exist. But that's what it feels like.

I look down at my wellingtons, sinking into the mud, then see the mud pooled in my juicer, my breadmaker, my percolator. Everything in drooping cardboard boxes, the marker pen still brightly exclaiming, in different splashes of colour "living room" or "kitchen", now soiled, useless, and filling me with disgust. My life, ready for a new start, now disposable.

The bright sunshine blinds me as I push a wheelbarrow up the ramp of the skip. I know what Sisyphus feels like. As I stand, knee deep in soaking, squalid personal effects, my familiar items jostling against a stranger's, I wipe my forehead with the crook of my elbow, not wanting to remove work-gloves, only to have to struggle putting them back on again. I stare at what other people have had to throw out; what these possessions might have meant, or what life they were awaiting as they reposed in storage, and now, swollen, silted and fetid, they are just so much rubbish. The cold is beginning to seep into my feet through my wellingtons, as I stand in flood-soaked detritus.

And it is, once again, starting to rain.

Redcap

The boys ran on ahead, shouting with delight at finding a carpet of fly agaric toadstools. They were still young enough to believe that they were magical, or pixie houses. I had always found them slightly malevolent, after my dad had told me about the murderous goblins called redcaps. Their caps, looking not unlike the domes of the fly agaric, would be dipped in the blood of their victims, and glisten. Their hats were their life. They needed them bloodied, or they would die.

"The most notorious redcap," my father had said, "was a familiar of a Laird who conspired against Robert the Bruce. He was dragged into the centre of a stone circle and boiled to death. Redcaps live along the Border. You often get demons along borders – it's all about edges, uncertainties, things going one way or another. That's where all the legends about full moons and new moons come from. Balance, you know."

I had nodded, absorbing the information but not really engaging. My father told me stories all the time, and sometimes my attention was caught by them. I tried, unsuccessfully, to put the redcap out of my mind, as, like the doff-off goblin, it sounded like a creature that would haunt my nightmares if I let it.

"The redcaps," he went on, "would track a traveller. You would hear the heavy tread of their iron boots, but when you turned around, they would be concealed, hidden. On you would go, the fear and uncertainty building in you. You would hear their sharp talons scratching along the stone wall, and you would stop, spin round to catch a glimpse of who was following you, but again... nothing. Imagine," he said, "imagine your building terror. Imagine this invisible assailant; you know it is there, you know it means you harm, you know it is going to end in your demise, but it is keeping you waiting, waiting, until your blood is rushing with fear, your heart is pounding, your breath is catching... and then slash!"

I jumped.

"Slash! Stab! The redcap's talons slice you open! The blood is pouring out. The redcap waits until you sink to the ground, lost and alone along the border, and he kneels on your chest, drinks deep from the wound he has caused, and dips his cap in your blood. The last thing your dying eyes see is his red cap contrasting with the green grass. Like those fly agarics."

He pointed, and I followed the gesture. The group of fungi looked like a gang of ghastly gnomes, bowed over, plotting together, watching... I shuddered, and scowled at dad, who was grinning at my discomfort.

We had continued our walk through the forest, but my imagination was supplying the rhythmic thud of iron boots, and evil, tracking goblins. Each toadstool became more malevolent than just a toxic fungus, and I was glad to break out into the clearing. Of course my nightmares were riddled by long fingers with talons reaching out from the darkness, and blood dripping from sharp-toothed maws. But the true nightmare was still to come.

Years later, when our walks had started to become slower, but still taking in forests and stories, I noticed a clump of fly agarics and pointed them out. Dad nodded, then was overtaken by another coughing fit, which were becoming more frequent. He looked distressed, and spat his phlegm out on the ground. A gobbet of blood-tainted froth stood proud against the deep green of the grass, sitting beside the hoods of agarics. I looked in horror, and asked the wordless question with my tear-brimming eyes. Dad took his handkerchief out, wiped his mouth, and answered my question without words.

The concealed goblin stalked him relentlessly for a few years. In and out of hospitals. In and out of our hopes, and our fears. And although it finally caught up with him, my dad never had to travel alone in his last days, never had to be afraid. When he crossed the border, the demons did not claim their victim.

"Don't touch those toadstools!" I yelled at the boys.

"It's all right, mummy," said the oldest one. "We won't knock his hat off"

"What do you mean?" I asked.

"The goblin. We won't knock his hat off. He needs it or he won't live"

The boys looked slightly past me, with that unnerving way that children have of seeing something or someone just behind you. I refused to look round, but uncharacteristically kicked the tops off the toadstools, then took the boys quickly away.

Taxing

He put down the six Scrabble tiles with a look that managed to be both sheepish and triumphant.

"'Taxing'. And it's on a triple word score. Sorry. 52 is that?"

She smiled thinly. At least she had got rid of the J and was only left with the Q and the Z to count up in the final score. Unless a miracle occurred.

"I don't know why we always have to play Scrabble. I can never concentrate" she said, not for the first time. ("Or care," she added, privately.)

"Well… it passes the time" he replied, absorbed in the board. She bit back retorts about other ways to pass the time, feeling decidedly against any physical ways of doing this, as they alternately cooked and froze in the dank tent.

"Let's just jump on a bus and go somewhere" he had suggested, brandishing a leaflet for Reay's buses. "Look, there's York Minster, or Alton Towers. Or Corrie! We could see if there are any good places to camp in the area – York must have camp sites…"

"I think these are just day trips", she said, prising the leaflet out of his fingers, and trying to keep the relief out of her voice.

"Oh right. Well, how about we jump on a train..." he rummaged a battered street atlas of Cumbria out from under the sofa... "we could go down to Kendal, or is it Oxenholme where you get off for the Lakes? Just us and a tent. We could do some walking."

She had shrugged, non-committally, which was why she was now fighting exhaustion, having carried a huge pack from platform to camp-site. His back had seized up on the train, so the lion's share of luggage had fallen to her. He looked at his watch.

"12.30. Probably time to put the torches off and turn in"

She nodded, and unwrapped her earplugs from the receipt she had stored them in. Dark chocolate from the World Shop, which he had eaten, saying he hadn't realised it was a treat. She popped the earplugs in, hoping they would guard against the worst of the snores, seeing as he needed to sleep on his back now, "to see if it loosens up." Like a comfy bed in a guest-house wouldn't have been a better option.

Rising early (or barely sleeping, with the cold, the snores and the whiffling fart of the deflating airbed), she scrambled out of the tent. The strange damp chill of the air made her nostrils prickle, and her skin feel greasy. She felt the nudge of the key in her concealed pocket, with its little blue keyring, like the Madonna's dress.

"Any time you need an escape," he had said as he'd handed it to her. "*Any* time."

She wondered if this was that time.

Donna Browne

Donna joined Carlisle Writers in 2012 and finds the support and encouragement of the group inspiring. She had been writing since her teens and returned to it in 2011 when she found it helped her cope with the loss of her mother.

Donna was born in Carlisle and returned to the city in 2009 after living abroad, where her husband was stationed with the army for ten years. She now lives in Botcherby with her family.

According To Legend

Through an open window, no breeze came. On a hot and humid night, moonlight illuminated the crinkled, white bed sheets and a restless figure. A mound of blonde curls fanned out upon a pillow. A digital alarm clock on the night stand read three thirty. In the dimness, augmented by the clock's light, stood a single white rose in a flute of water. Some distance from the bed, blinking blue eyes admired the flower's beauty, its purity and its meaning.

She had found it placed upon the desk in her English lecture. After realizing she had forgotten to pick up her text book after class, Kayley Carson had gone back to collect it. It lay on the face of Shakespeare's *Romeo and Juliet*, a magical, alluring shine all of its own. Just her book and the rose had been left. No note, no clue, no nothing.

Although Kayley had had a feeling of being watched for some time over the past few weeks, she wasn't scared. In fact she knew to whom those watchful eyes belonged. She had watchful eyes of her own.

Kayley couldn't sleep and it wasn't like she hadn't tried. She knew that the summer heat was not to blame. It was a different kind of heat, the kind that ran through her veins, set her heart racing and gave her butterflies in her stomach.

According to legend, if you can't sleep at night it's because you're awake in someone else's dream.

Kayley could only wish that this was true - and wish it she did! The truth was Aaron Matthews was out of her league. Handsome, popular, out-going, extremely intelligent and incredibly rich. All the things she wasn't and everything she desired to be. The only sure thing was he'd been watching her a lot lately and her insecurities screamed, 'Stupid girl, if he liked you, he'd have had you already.' Because that was the kind of man he was and the idea of there ever being anything between them was starting to seem ludicrous.

Ten minutes later Kayley was sitting at her desk, her face illuminated by the computer screen. Defeated, she carelessly flicked through the pages of a social networking site. The same old Friday night updates of parties, fall outs, hook-ups, drunken posts and cringe-worthy photos filled the screen. Kayley chose to stay home that night, like she did every night. Not because she didn't want to go out and have fun with friends, but because she couldn't afford to. University and twelve-hour shifts at the local fish factory at weekends kept her schedule full and social life empty.

When Lady Gaga's *Poker Face* ring tone broke the eerie silence of the mould-infested bedsit that Kayley rented, she found was half way across the room on her computer chair before reality registered.

"Hello," she said, trying to hide her nerves. The number was unfamiliar. Although she was anxious, hope and excitement resurfaced.

"Kayley?" the voice replied. Deep, husky and masculine, it was definitely a man calling.

Her heart skipping a beat, Kayley's voice caught as she replied in a pathetic squeak.

A low chuckle tickled her ear. "I was just calling to see if you liked my surprise?" he whispered, letting the question linger.

When Kayley didn't answer - because she couldn't - he laughed, louder this time, and harder.

On the screen in front of her was the image of a girl with blonde hair falling freely down her back. A white silk nightdress was clinging to her sweaty body; you couldn't tell from the picture, but Kayley knew this to be true. How? Because the girl in the picture was her and the person on the phone wasn't Aaron. The man reflected in the mirror in front of her was someone Kayley had never seen before.

According to legend, if you can't sleep at night it is because you are awake in someone else's dream.

What they don't tell you is that it can be exactly the opposite: you're awake in a nightmare that is entirely your own.

215

Raindrop

Raindrop, in the morning dew,
reminds me of how I miss you,
when off to heaven you just flew,
making me wish I could fly there too.

Raindrop, on the window pane.
A matching teardrop I sought to detain,
trying not to hate and blame
when they refused to start your heart again.

Raindrop, dark and blue.
A storm inside me starts to brew;
saving life is what they're supposed to do.
They're breaking the golden rule.

Raindrop, crystal clear,
a whisper from heaven that calms all fear:
to call your name and you will hear.
You may be gone, but you're always near.

Aftermath

I'm the monster that comes after;
the second wave of attack.
The plague behind the disaster,
the cold shiver that runs down your back.

I'm the haunting echo of the Twin Towers,
the timeless horror still fresh to mind.
The pain hidden in bitter-sweet memorial flowers,
the closure they'll never find.

I'm the reality of every parents' worst nightmare,
the Executioner dictating that they failed.
I'm the number of Interpol's missing,
swimming in their despair;
the injustice of predators who never get jailed.

I'm the anxiety engulfing the soldier's terror,
the movie reel in his own hell.
I'm the blanket suffocating him in fear,
the wheel chair of the man who fell.

I'm the fuel that ignites depression,
the soulless skeleton of a broken person, a shattered home.
The genesis of the therapy session,
the hell on earth, the battle done.

Who am I?

I am everything and yet nothing,
the destiny to your chosen path.
I'm the absent referee in life's boxing ring,
the unstoppable Aftermath.

Other books by Carlisle Writers, available from Amazon and elsewhere.

Write On! Carlisle Writers' Group's previous anthology

Trisha's Fishy Tales and Bugs On The Go by Trisha Nelson

In Another Life & Daisy Chain by Roberta Twentyman

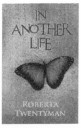

(also available from major UK bookshops)

Brandon & Bailey by Hayley Cordley

(also available from major UK bookshops)

Short & Curly and *Why Christians Don't Do What Jesus Tells Them To ...And What They Believe Instead* by Neil Robinson

A Sting In The Tale by John Nevinson

Copies of this book, as well as the Kindle version, can be purchased on Amazon at

http://www.amazon.co.uk/s/ref=nb_sb_noss?url=search-alias%3Dstripbooks&field-keywords=carlisle%20writers

or search 'Carlisle Writers'.

33204094R00127

Made in the USA
Charleston, SC
07 September 2014